PHYSICS REVISION FOR LEAVING CERTIFICATE

PHYSICS REVISION

FOR

LEAVING CERTIFICATE

BRENDAN CASSERLY
AND
BERNARD HORGAN

GILL & MACMILLAN

Gill & Macmillan Ltd
Hume Avenue
Park West
Dublin 12
with associated companies throughout the world
www.gillmacmillan.ie

© Brendan Casserly and Bernard Horgan 2002
0 7171 3375 3

Print origination in Ireland by
Carrigboy Typesetting Services, County Cork.

The paper used in this book is made from the wood pulp of managed forests.
For every tree felled, at least one tree is planted, thereby renewing natural resources.

Contents

Introduction

The difference between an average mark and a good mark in physics often comes down to one thing – attention to detail – **so please read the following introduction carefully**! The new format examination paper for the new physics course contains four questions based on mandatory experiments. It is very easy to lose marks in these questions so take note of the following:

1. Never describe an experiment without a **labelled** diagram.
2. The instructions for doing the experiment should be given in 6 or 7 separate points rather than in a block of text.
3. Each point should, where possible, consist of a single sentence.
4. Be aware of the concept of **percentage error**. If you are measuring something which is 10 cm long and you make an error of 1 cm then the percentage error is 10%. However, if you are measuring something which is 1 m long and you make an error of 1 cm then the percentage error is only 1%. So, if you can, design your experiment so that the quantities you measure are as big as possible.
5. **Graphs**
   When drawing a graph always label each axis clearly stating what each axis represents and the units in which it is measured.

   If you are given a table of readings and asked to draw a **suitable** graph this usually means that the appropriate graph cannot be drawn from the given table. For example, in refraction of light if you are given a table of i against r you must use the readings in that table to draw up a table of **sin i** against **sin r**.

   Choose a scale that makes your graph as big as possible so as to reduce percentage error when taking readings from the graph.

   If the calculations involve a fraction, e.g. $\frac{\sin i}{\sin r}$, put the top of the fraction on the vertical axis and the bottom on the horizontal axis.

   The most useful type of graph is a straight-line graph. If some of the points are out of line then draw the line of best fit.

   A straight line through the origin shows that the two quantities being graphed are directly proportional to each other.

   In getting the slope of the graph choose two convenient points as far apart as possible so as to maximise your figures and minimise any percentage error.

   If plotting two particular quantities, e.g. P against V, gives a graph which is not a straight line it may be possible to plot two associated quantities such as P against $\frac{1}{V}$ to get a more convenient straight-line graph.

   To illustrate some of the above points consider the following question:

   The following results were obtained by a student in an experiment to measure, g, the acceleration due to gravity using a simple pendulum.

Length (l) in metres	0·2	0·4	0·6	0·8	1·0	1·2	1·4	1·6
Time (T) for 30 oscillations in seconds	27·0	37·8	46·5	53·7	60·6	66·0	70·8	76·4

Draw a **suitable** graph and hence determine the value of g.

This question involves a formula since $g = \frac{4\pi^2 l}{T^2}$. You must plot a graph of l against T^2.

The slope of this graph will give you a value for $\frac{l}{T^2}$. Multiply this by $4\pi^2$ to get g.

Start by dividing each figure in the bottom line of your table by 30 to get T, the time for 1 oscillation. Then square each answer to get T^2. Now draw your graph, etc.

6. **Mandatory experiments**

It is important to realise which experiments are mandatory and which are not although several non-mandatory experiments also appear on examination papers. The mandatory experiments are:

To find the focal length of a concave mirror.
To verify Snell's law.
To find the refractive index of a rectangular glass block.
To find the refractive index of a liquid.
To find the focal length of a converging lens.
To measure the wavelength of monochromatic light using a diffraction grating.
To measure the velocity of sound using a resonance tube.
To investigate the variation of the fundamental frequency of a string with length.
• To investigate the variation of the fundamental frequency of a string with tension.
• To investigate the relationship between period and length for a simple pendulum and hence to calculate g.
To measure g by free fall.
To show that acceleration is proportional to force ($a \propto F$).
To verify the principle of conservation of momentum.
To measure the velocity of a body.
To measure the acceleration of a body.
To investigate the laws of equilibrium for a set of coplanar forces.
To draw the calibration curve of a thermometer using a mercury thermometer as a standard.
To verify Boyle's law.
To find the specific heat capacity of a metal.
To find the specific heat capacity of a liquid.
To find the specific latent heat of fusion of ice.
To find the specific latent heat of vaporisation of water.
To investigate how the current flowing through various conductors varies with the potential difference applied.
To measure the resistivity of the material of a wire.
To investigate how the resistance of a metallic conductor varies with temperature.
To investigate how the resistance of a thermistor varies with temperature.
To verify Joule's law.

Bulleted points are honours experiments. Note that honours material including experiments is marked in the text with a mariginal line.

Finally, when putting numbers into formulae, remember that they must be in standard units: 2 minutes must be 120 seconds, 20 cm must be 0·2 m, etc.

Chapter 1 – Reflection of Light

Light is reflected according to the laws of reflection.

1. **The angle of reflection (r) is equal to the angle of incidence (i).**
2. **The incident ray, the normal and the reflected ray are all in the same plane.**
   (All three can be drawn on a flat sheet of paper.)

Note that the angle of incidence (i) is between the incident ray and the normal, not between the incident ray and the mirror.

The image we see in a plane mirror is caused by reflection from the back of the mirror as you can see from Figure 1.1. The rays of light entering the eye seem to come from behind the mirror so that is where the image is seen.

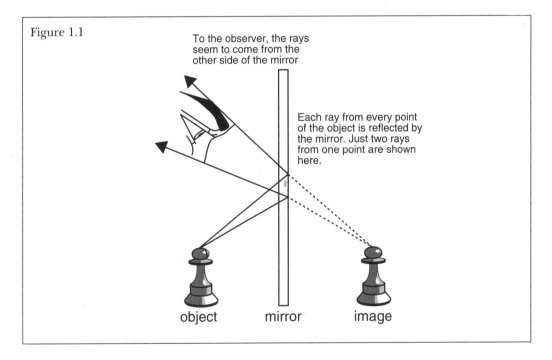

Figure 1.1

To the observer, the rays seem to come from the other side of the mirror

Each ray from every point of the object is reflected by the mirror. Just two rays from one point are shown here.

object   mirror   image

Parallax is the apparent relative movement of two objects due to the movement of the observer.

There are two kinds of image, real and virtual:

A real image is formed by the **actual** intersection of light rays. It is always **inverted** and can be formed on a screen.

A virtual image is formed by the **apparent** intersection of light rays. It is always **erect** and cannot be formed on a screen.

Images formed in plane mirrors are virtual, laterally inverted, the same size as the object and as far behind the mirror as the object is in front.

SPHERICAL MIRRORS

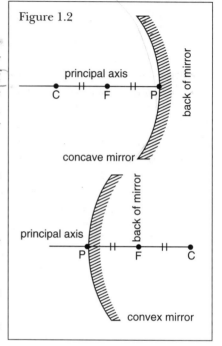

Figure 1.2

There are two types of curved mirror, concave and convex. If you look into the front of a highly polished spoon you will see an image of yourself upside down. You are looking into a **concave** mirror. If you look into the back of the spoon you will see an image of yourself the right way up. You are now looking into a **convex** mirror.

Does that actully happen?

P is called the pole of the mirror. C is the centre of curvature. F is the focus. FP is the focal length. CP is the radius of curvature. CP = 2 FP

Rays of light are reflected from a concave mirror according to the following rules:

1. Rays of light parallel to the principal axis are reflected back through the focus.
2. Rays of light passing through the focus are reflected parallel to the principal axis.
3. Rays of light coming from the direction of the centre of curvature are reflected back along their own path.

The position, nature (real or virtual) and size of an image depends on the distance of the object from the mirror, as the following ray diagrams in Figure 1.3 show.

Figure 1.3

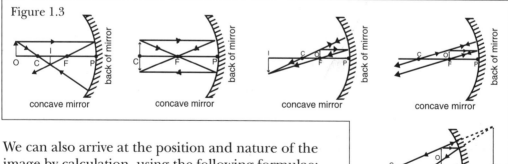

concave mirror   concave mirror   concave mirror   concave mirror

We can also arrive at the position and nature of the image by calculation, using the following formulae:

$$\frac{1}{f} = \frac{1}{u} + \frac{1}{v} \text{ and } m = \frac{v}{u}$$

f = focal length, u = distance from mirror to object, v = distance from mirror to image, m = the magnification

SIGN CONVENTION

For a real image we take v as positive. For a virtual image v is negative. Focal length is positive for a concave mirror and negative for a convex mirror.

MANDATORY EXPERIMENT

AIM: TO FIND THE FOCAL LENGTH OF A CONCAVE MIRROR.

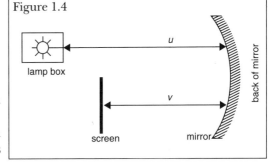

Figure 1.4

Method

1. Set up the apparatus as shown in Figure 1.4.
2. Adjust the position of the screen until a sharp image of the slit is formed on it.
3. Measure u and v.
4. Calculate the focal length from the formula $\dfrac{1}{f} = \dfrac{1}{u} + \dfrac{1}{v}$

5. Repeat for different positions of the lamp box and find the average value of f.

Rays of light are reflected from a convex mirror according to the following rules:

1. Rays parallel to the principal axis are reflected so as to appear to be coming from the focus.
2. Rays of light heading toward the centre of curvature are reflected back along their own path.

When an object is placed in front of a convex mirror, the image is always virtual, erect and diminished.

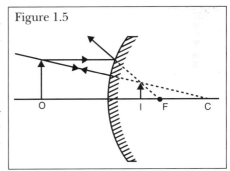

Figure 1.5

Problem 1

An object is placed 15 cm in front of a concave mirror of focal length 10 cm. Find the position, magnification and nature of the image.

$$\frac{1}{f} = \frac{1}{u} + \frac{1}{v} \ \Rightarrow\ \frac{1}{10} = \frac{1}{15} + \frac{1}{v} \ \Rightarrow\ \frac{1}{10} - \frac{1}{15} = \frac{1}{v} \ \Rightarrow\ \frac{1}{30} = \frac{1}{v}$$

$$\Rightarrow v = 30 \text{ cm}$$

(v is positive as the image is real)

$$m = \frac{v}{u} = \frac{30}{15} = 2$$

Answer: A real, inverted image, twice the size of the object, 30 cm from the mirror.

Problem 2

A convex mirror of focal length 12 cm forms an image 4 cm from the mirror. Find the position of the object.

$f = -12$ cm, $v = -4$ cm (why negative?), $u = ?$

$$\frac{1}{f} = \frac{1}{u} + \frac{1}{v} \implies \frac{1}{-12} = \frac{1}{u} + \frac{1}{-4} \implies \frac{1}{4} - \frac{1}{12} = \frac{1}{u} \qquad \frac{3}{12} - \frac{1}{12} = \frac{1}{u}$$

$$\frac{1}{6} = \frac{1}{u}$$

$u = 6$ cm

The object is 6 cm in front of the mirror.

Problem 3

An object placed 20 cm in front of a concave mirror has a real image 3 times the height of the object. Where must the object be placed to form a virtual image 3 times the height of the object?

Stage 1

$u = 20$ cm, $m = 3 \implies \frac{v}{u} = 3 \implies \frac{v}{20} = 3 \implies v = 60$ cm

$$\frac{1}{f} = \frac{1}{u} + \frac{1}{v}$$

$$\frac{1}{f} = \frac{1}{20} + \frac{1}{60}$$

$$\frac{1}{f} = \frac{4}{60} = \frac{1}{15}$$

$f = 15$ cm

Stage 2

$f = 15$ cm, $u = ?$, $v = ?$, $m = 3$

$m = 3 \quad \frac{v}{u} = 3 \quad v = 3u$

However, since the image is virtual v is negative.

$$\frac{1}{15} = \frac{1}{u} - \frac{1}{3u} \implies \frac{1}{15} = \frac{2}{3u} \implies 3u = 30 \implies u = 10 \text{ cm}$$

The object must be placed 10 cm in front of the mirror.

USES OF CONCAVE MIRRORS

Concave mirrors are used as reflectors in car headlamps, flashlights, electric bar heaters etc.

As concave mirrors give a magnified erect image they can also be used as shaving and make-up mirrors but be sure your face is inside the focus. (Why?)

A dentist uses specially designed concave mirrors to examine your teeth.

USES OF CONVEX MIRRORS

Convex mirrors have two advantages:

1. The images formed by convex mirrors are always erect, not inverted.
2. Convex mirrors provide a large field of view. Convex mirrors of very long focal length (they could be mistaken for plane mirrors) are used as wing mirrors in cars because they give a wide field of view without giving a false sense of distance.

Convex mirrors are also used on buses, in shops and at dangerous junctions because they can, in effect, enable us to see round corners.

SUMMARY

- Light is a form of energy.
- The laws of reflection are:
  1. The angle of reflection (r) is equal to the angle of incidence (i)
  2. The incident ray, the normal and the reflected ray are all in the same plane.
- A real image is formed by the actual intersection of light rays. It can be formed on a screen and is always inverted.
- A virtual image is formed by the apparent intersection of rays. It cannot be formed on a screen and is always erect.
- A concave mirror forms a virtual image when the object is inside the focus.
- $\frac{1}{f} = \frac{1}{u} + \frac{1}{v}$
- $m = \frac{v}{u}$
- Concave mirrors are used as reflectors in headlamps, as make-up mirrors and by dentists.
- Convex mirrors give a wide field of view and are used as rear-view mirrors in cars, in buses, shops and at dangerous junctions.

Chapter 2 – Refraction of Light

Refraction means that light bends when it passes from one medium to another medium of different density.

When it passes into a denser medium (e.g. from air to water) the light slows down.

(You should remember from Junior Certificate science that light belongs to a group of waves called the electromagnetic spectrum. As for all waves, velocity = frequency × wavelength. In this case the light slows down because the **wavelength decreases**, the frequency remains the same.

Laws of Refraction

1. $\dfrac{\sin i}{\sin r}$ **is constant for two given media.**
   (This is called Snell's law.)

2. **The incident ray, the refracted ray and the normal are all in the same plane.**

$\dfrac{\sin i}{\sin r}$ is known as the refractive index n

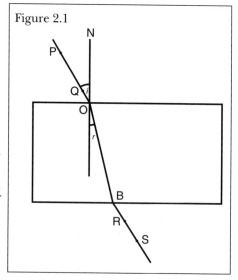

Figure 2.1

MANDATORY EXPERIMENT

AIM: TO VERIFY SNELL'S LAW.

Method

1. Draw the outline of a glass block on a sheet of paper. Remove the block.
2. Draw a normal NO to the side of the block and a line making an angle of incidence of 20° with NO. Replace the block. Stick two pins P and Q on the line, as in Figure 2.1.
3. Stick two pins R and S in line with the images of P and Q as seen through the block. Remove block and pins.
4. Join RS and continue it on until it meets the outline of the block at B. Join OB. Measure the angle of refraction r.
5. Repeat this procedure for angles of incidence of 30°, 40° etc. and plot a graph of **sin i** against **sin r.**

Result: The result should be a straight line through the origin which verifies Snell's law.

Refraction can produce some curious effects as you can see from Figure 2.2.

In Figure 2.2 $\dfrac{\text{real depth}}{\text{apparent depth}} = \dfrac{4}{3}$ which is in fact the refractive index of water.

This gives us an alternative method of finding the refractive index.

Refractive Index $= \dfrac{\textbf{real depth}}{\textbf{apparent depth}}$

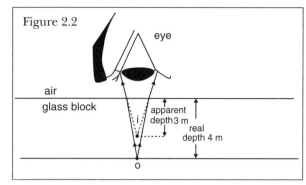

Figure 2.2

MANDATORY EXPERIMENT

AIM: TO FIND THE REFRACTIVE INDEX OF A RECTANGULAR GLASS BLOCK.

Method

1. Draw a straight line on a sheet of paper.
2. Stand a glass block on end over the line.
3. Move the search pin up and down until it coincides, without parallax, with the image of the line as seen in the block.
4. Fix the search pin to the side of the block and measure the apparent depth.
5. Now measure the real depth of the block.
6. The refractive index $= \dfrac{\text{real depth}}{\text{apparent depth}}$

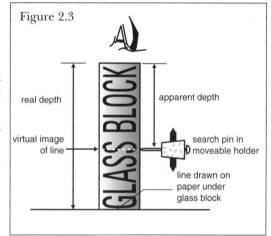

Figure 2.3

MANDATORY EXPERIMENT

AIM: TO FIND THE REFRACTIVE INDEX OF A LIQUID.

Method

1. Set up the apparatus as shown in the diagram.
2. Move the search pin up and down until it coincides, without parallax, with the image of the line as seen in the liquid.
3. Fix the search pin to the side of the beaker and measure the apparent depth.
4. Measure the real depth of the beaker.
5. Refractive index $= \dfrac{\text{real depth}}{\text{apparent depth}}$

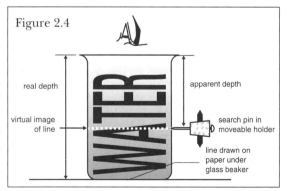

Figure 2.4

Problem 1

A rectangular glass block has a real width of 6 cm and an apparent width of 4 cm. What is the refractive index of the block? If the block is 3 cm deep, by how much will the print over which it is placed appear to be raised?

$n = \dfrac{6}{4} = \dfrac{3}{2} = 1\cdot5$ $\dfrac{3}{x} = \dfrac{3}{2}$ $x = 2$ **Answer: 1 cm** *how did they → get 1*
Thought the answer was 2?! & I can only get 2. help..

When finding the refractive index for two media, neither of which is air, use the following formula:

    Refractive index from medium 1 to medium 3 = (index from 1 to 2) × (index from 2 to 3).

Problem 2

The refractive index for glass is $\dfrac{3}{2}$ and the refractive index for water is $\dfrac{4}{3}$. What is the refractive index from water to glass?

$_a n_w = \dfrac{4}{3}$ so $_w n_a = \dfrac{3}{4}$

$_w n_g = {_w}n_a \times {_a}n_g = \dfrac{3}{4} \times \dfrac{3}{2} = \dfrac{9}{8}$

TOTAL INTERNAL REFLECTION

Total internal reflection can only occur when light passes into a less dense medium and can be demonstrated as shown in Figure 2.5.

When light passes from glass to air it is refracted away from the normal as in diagram (a). As the angle of incidence is increased the angle of refraction eventually reaches 90° as in diagram (b). If the angle of incidence increases beyond this value total internal reflection occurs as in diagram (c).

The critical angle *(C)* is the angle of incidence in the denser medium corresponding to an angle of refraction of 90° in the less dense medium.

From diagram (b) the refractive index from air to glass

$n = \dfrac{\sin 90}{\sin C} \Rightarrow n = \dfrac{1}{\sin C}$

As the refractive index of glass is $\dfrac{3}{2}$

$\dfrac{3}{2} = \dfrac{1}{\sin C}$ $\sin C = \dfrac{2}{3} = 0\cdot667 \Rightarrow C = 41°49'$

The critical angle for glass is 41°49'.

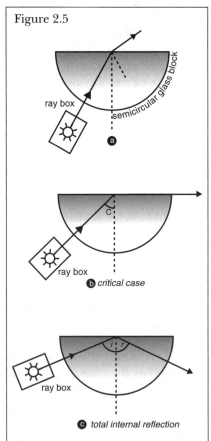

Figure 2.5

ray box

semicircular glass block

(a)

ray box

(b) *critical case*

C

ray box

(c) *total internal reflection*

i   r

Total internal reflection occurs when the angle of incidence in the denser medium is greater than the critical angle.

Problem

Find the critical angle for water if the refractive index of water is $\frac{4}{3}$.

$$n = \frac{1}{\sin C} \Rightarrow \sin C = \frac{1}{n} \Rightarrow \sin C = \frac{3}{4} \Rightarrow C = 48°35'$$

APPLICATIONS

Total internal reflection has some very useful applications. To begin with glass prisms can be used to turn a ray of light through 90°, 180°and other angles. This can be used in the periscope and in binoculars.

1. Periscope

High quality periscopes use prisms instead of mirrors because prisms give total internal reflection and are not prone to deterioration like mirrors.

2. Prism binoculars

The size of the final image in a pair of binoculars depends on the distance travelled by the light within the binoculars. By using two prisms this distance can be increased without increasing the length of the binoculars.

3. Fibre optics

An optical fibre consists of a hair-like thread of glass surrounded by an outer layer of less dense glass. Light is trapped within the core by total internal reflection as shown in Figure 2.6. Using optical fibres light can be piped from one place to another in much the same way as water.

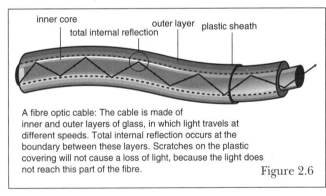

A fibre optic cable: The cable is made of inner and outer layers of glass, in which light travels at different speeds. Total internal reflection occurs at the boundary between these layers. Scratches on the plastic covering will not cause a loss of light, because the light does not reach this part of the fibre.

Figure 2.6

In the communications industry fibre optic cables are being used to replace conventional telephone cables. Another application is the **endoscope**. One bundle of optical fibres, called a light guide, carries light into the patient's body. Another bundle of optical fibres, called the image guide, carries light back from inside the body to the observer. The endoscope has been used very effectively to examine and photograph the digestive system, reproductive system and the tubes leading to the heart. It has made a great deal of exploratory surgery unnecessary.

Problem

Use a diagram to show how a prism may be used to reflect light through an angle of 90°. Calculate the minimum value of the refractive index of the material of the prism for this to occur.

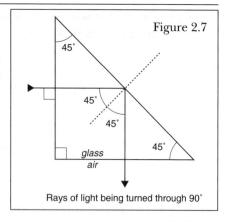

Figure 2.7

Rays of light being turned through 90°

Minimum refractive index $\Rightarrow$ maximum critical angle that in this case is 45°.

$$n = \frac{1}{\sin C} = \frac{1}{\sin 45°} = 1 \cdot 414$$

The reason why light bends when going from one medium to another is because of a change in velocity. This gives us another way of looking at refractive index.

Refractive index from medium 1 to medium 2 $= \dfrac{\text{velocity in medium 1}}{\text{velocity in medium 2}}$ $(n = \dfrac{C_1}{C_2})$

Problem

The speed of light in air is 3×10^8 m s^{-1}. If the refractive index of water is $\frac{4}{3}$ find the speed of light in water.

$$n = \frac{C_1}{C_2} \Rightarrow C_2 = \frac{C_1}{n} \Rightarrow C_2 = (3 \times 10^8) \times \frac{3}{4} = 2 \cdot 25 \times 10^8 \text{ m s}^{-1}$$

SUMMARY

- Refraction: light bends when it passes from one medium to another medium of different density.
- Laws of refraction:
    1. $\dfrac{\sin i}{\sin r}$ is constant for two given media.
    2. The incident ray, refracted ray and normal are all in the same plane.

- $n = \dfrac{\sin i}{\sin r} = \dfrac{\text{real depth}}{\text{apparent depth}} = \dfrac{\text{velocity in medium 1}}{\text{velocity in medium 2}}$

- The critical angle is the angle of incidence in the denser medium corresponding to an angle of refraction of 90° in the less dense medium.

- $n = \dfrac{1}{\sin c}$

- Total internal reflection occurs when the angle of incidence in the denser medium is greater than the critical angle.

- Total internal reflection is used in periscopes, prism binoculars, reflectors, fibre optics (communication and endoscopes).

Chapter 3 – Lenses

The diagram shows two common types of lens, **converging** (convex) and **diverging** (concave).

When drawing ray diagrams for converging lenses remember that:

1. **Rays of light parallel to the principal axis are refracted through F, the focus (and vice versa).**
2. **Rays passing through the centre of the lens are not deviated.**

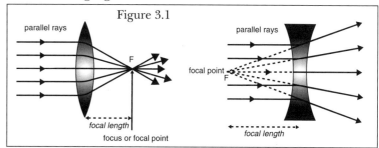

Figure 3.1

The position, nature and size of the image formed by a converging lens depends on the distance of the object from the lens, as you can see from the ray diagrams.

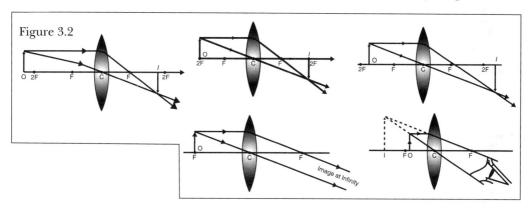

Figure 3.2

In the case of a diverging lens the image is always virtual, erect and diminished as shown in Figure 3.3.

Problems involving lenses can be solved by accurate ray diagrams or by using these formulae:

$$\frac{1}{f} = \frac{1}{u} + \frac{1}{v} \quad \text{and} \quad m = \frac{v}{u}$$

Sign convention: For a converging lens f is positive. For a diverging lens f is negative.

For a real image v is positive. For a virtual image v is negative.

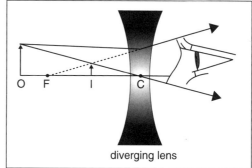

diverging lens

Problem 1

An object is placed 12 cm from a converging lens of focal length 10 cm. Find the position, nature and size of the image.

$$\frac{1}{f} = \frac{1}{u} + \frac{1}{v} \Rightarrow \frac{1}{10} = \frac{1}{12} + \frac{1}{v} \Rightarrow \frac{1}{10} - \frac{1}{12} = \frac{1}{v}$$

$$\Rightarrow \frac{6}{60} - \frac{5}{60} = \frac{1}{v}$$

$$\Rightarrow \frac{1}{60} = \frac{1}{v}$$

$$\Rightarrow v = 60$$

$$m = \frac{v}{u} = \frac{60}{12} = 5$$

A real image 5 times the size of the object is formed 60 cm from the lens.

Problem 2

A diverging lens of focal length 15 cm forms an image 5 cm from the lens. Find the position of the object.

Diverging lens so *f* is negative. Virtual image so *v* is negative.

$$\frac{1}{f} = \frac{1}{u} + \frac{1}{v} \Rightarrow \frac{1}{-15} = \frac{1}{u} + \frac{1}{-5} \Rightarrow \frac{1}{5} - \frac{1}{15} = \frac{1}{u}$$

$$\Rightarrow \frac{3}{15} - \frac{1}{15} = \frac{1}{u}$$

$$\Rightarrow \frac{2}{15} = \frac{1}{u}$$

$$\Rightarrow 7.5 = u$$

Answer: 7·5 cm from the lens.

Problem 3

An object and a screen are 60 cm apart. A converging lens placed between them gives an image on the screen three times the size of the object. Find the focal length of the lens. Also find a second position of the lens to give an image on the screen and calculate its size.

$$\frac{u}{v} = 3 \Rightarrow u = 3v \Rightarrow u + v = 60 \Rightarrow 3v + v = 60 \Rightarrow v = 15 \quad u = 45$$

$$\frac{1}{f} = \frac{1}{v} + \frac{1}{u} \Rightarrow \frac{1}{f} = \frac{1}{15} + \frac{1}{45} \Rightarrow \frac{1}{f} = \frac{4}{45} \Rightarrow f = 11·25 \text{ cm}$$

Interchange *u* and *v*. Lens is now 5 cm from screen. Magnification $= \frac{v}{u} = \frac{1}{3}$

MANDATORY EXPERIMENT

AIM: TO FIND THE FOCAL LENGTH OF A CONVERGING LENS.

Method

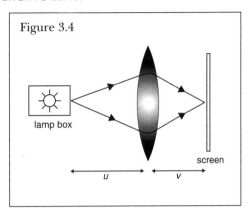

Figure 3.4

1. Set up the apparatus as shown in Figure 3.4.
2. Adjust the position of the lens until a sharp image of the slit in the lamp box is formed on the screen.
3. Measure u and v.
4. Calculate f from the formula $\dfrac{1}{f} = \dfrac{1}{u} + \dfrac{1}{v}$.
5. Repeat for different positions of the lamp box and calculate the average value of f.

THE POWER OF A LENS

Opticians often speak about the power of a lens.

$$\text{power} = \frac{1}{\text{focal length in metres}} \quad \left(P = \frac{1}{f}\right)$$

The power of a lens is measured in **dioptres** so a converging lens of focal length 20 cm would have a power of $\dfrac{1}{0.2\text{ m}} = 5$ dioptres.

You will easily know a powerful converging lens, it is much thicker than the lenses you use for experiments.

Sometimes a compound lens is formed by placing two lenses of powers P_1 and P_2 in contact.

In this case $P = P_1 + P_2$ or $\dfrac{1}{F} = \dfrac{1}{f_1} + \dfrac{1}{f_2}$

SUMMARY

- A converging lens forms a virtual image when the object is inside the focus.
- A diverging lens always forms a virtual, erect, diminished image.
- For a converging lens f is positive.
- For a diverging lens f is negative.
- The power of a lens $P = \dfrac{1}{f}$.
- For two lenses in contact $P = P_1 + P_2$.

Chapter 4 – Helping the Eye

One of the main uses of lenses is to help compensate for defects in the human eye. When a perfect eye is relaxed, the distance from the lens to the retina is equal to the focal length of the lens. This means that rays of light from a distant object, which are practically parallel, are brought to a focus on the retina where a sharp image is formed. As the object moves closer to the eye the ciliary muscles cause the lens to bulge shortening its focal length so that the image is still formed on the retina. This process is called **accommodation**. When the object comes to a point about 25 cm from the eye the eye cannot accommodate any further. This is called the **near point** and the distance from this point to the eye is called the least distance of distinct vision. Any object closer to the eye than this distance cannot be seen properly. (Try this by holding a pencil at arm's length and bringing it slowly toward your eye.)

DEFECTS OF THE EYE

1. Myopia or short sight

The eyeball is too long for the lens so that light from a distant object is not brought to a focus on the retina. This means that distant objects cannot be seen clearly. The remedy is to place a suitable diverging lens in front of the eye as shown in Figure 4.1.

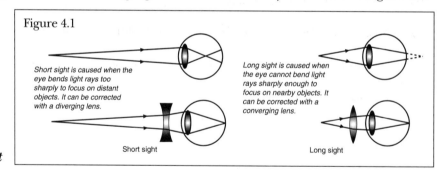

Figure 4.1

Short sight is caused when the eye bends light rays too sharply to focus on distant objects. It can be corrected with a diverging lens.

Long sight is caused when the eye cannot bend light rays sharply enough to focus on nearby objects. It can be corrected with a converging lens.

Short sight

Long sight

2. Long sight

In this case the eyeball is too short for the lens. The remedy is to place a suitable converging lens in front of the eye.

As people get older the lenses in their eyes become less flexible so they cannot change shape (focal length) as much as before. This can lead to problems with reading and also with distant vision. One solution is to have two pairs of glasses, one for general use and one for reading. Another solution is **bifocal lenses** with the top part for distant vision and the bottom part for reading.

Contact lenses

Many people prefer contact lenses to glasses. Contact lenses appear to be placed directly onto the cornea, but in fact a film of tear fluid forms between the lens and the eye and the lens is held in place by surface tension. They give better all-round vision than glasses but they must be properly cleaned to prevent eye infection.

The magnifying glass

Even if your eyes are perfect they may still need help. For example have you ever tried to read the fine detail on an ordnance survey map? If you have you know why so many students bring a magnifying glass into a geography exam.

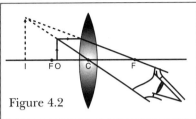

Figure 4.2

The magnifying glass is a converging lens of short focal length. The lens is held close to the object so that the object is inside the focus of the lens. The result is a virtual, erect and magnified image. The eye is placed close to the lens so that the image is at the near point thus giving the greatest magnification.

The microscope

The magnifying glass is fine for studying ordnance survey maps but would not do for blood cells. What we need in this case is a microscope. The first lens (the objective lens) forms an image inside the microscope. The microscope is adjusted so that this image is just inside the focus of the

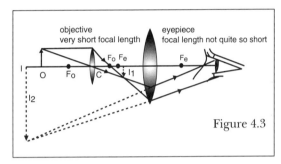

Figure 4.3

eyepiece lens. The eyepiece lens now acts as a magnifying glass and the final image is formed at the near point.

The astronomical telescope

A single lens cannot produce a magnified image of a distant object but two lenses can. This is what happens in a telescope. When the final image is formed at infinity it can be viewed with a relaxed eye thus avoiding eyestrain. The telescope is now in **normal adjustment**.

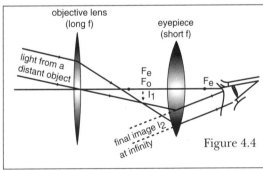

Figure 4.4

The spectrometer

A spectrometer is used to study light and is shown in Figure 4.5. It consists of:

1. A **collimator (C)** that is a tube with a slit (S) at one end and a converging lens at the other. In practice the slit should be at the focus of the lens so that light entering the slit will emerge from the lens as a parallel beam.
2. A **telescope (T)** with crosswires in its eyepiece.
3. A **circular scale** that is marked in degrees and has a vernier scale attached.
4. A **table** that rotates and can be levelled with three screws.

Before use the spectrometer must be adjusted as follows:

1. Adjust the eyepiece until the crosswires are clearly seen.
2. Focus the telescope on a distant object.
3. Place a lamp in front of the slit and place the telescope in line with the collimator.
4. Adjust the width of the slit to give a fairly narrow beam of light and adjust the telescope until the image of the slit coincides with the crosswires without parallax.
5. Level the table.

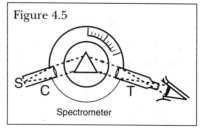

Figure 4.5

Spectrometer

The camera

Despite the fact that it can have the faults mentioned above, as well as others, the eye is a wonderful organ. In designing the camera, man has tried to copy the eye to some extent. There are, however, certain marked differences.

To begin with, a camera lens is rigid so the focal length cannot be changed: instead the light is focused on the film by moving the lens in or out.

The amount of light entering the camera is controlled in two ways:

1. The diaphragm can be adjusted to vary the size of the **aperture** through which the light passes. This is similar to the way in which the iris controls the amount of light entering the eye, although the iris is more flexible than the diaphragm.
2. The amount of light entering the camera can also be controlled by varying the amount of time the shutter remains open, i.e. the shutter speed.

Finally, the image formed on the film is permanent whereas the image formed on the retina is not.

SUMMARY

- Accommodation means that the eye focuses objects at different distances from it onto the retina by changing the shape, as well as the focal length, of the lens.
- A converging lens acts as a magnifying glass if the object is placed inside the focus.
- A simple microscope has two converging lenses of short focal length.
- An astronomical telescope has two converging lenses, an objective of long focal length and an eyepiece of short focal length.

Chapter 5 – Waves

Our main source of energy is the sun, but the sun's energy would be of little use to us if it could not travel from the sun to the earth. One very important way in which energy travels is by means of waves.

TYPES OF WAVES

Transverse waves are waves that travel perpendicular to the direction of vibration of the particles.

All the waves in the electromagnetic spectrum, including **light waves**, are transverse waves.

Longitudinal waves are waves that travel parallel to the direction of vibration of the particles.

Sound waves are longitudinal.

We can learn a great deal about waves by mathematical calculations and by experiments. For mathematical purposes waves may be represented as shown in Figure 5.1.

The **amplitude** (a) of a wave is the greatest displacement from rest.
The **frequency** (f) is the number of waves passing a fixed point per second.
One wave per second = 1 **hertz.**
The **wavelength** (λ) the distance from one crest to the next.

velocity = frequency × wavelength

$c = f \times \lambda$

This formula applies to **all** waves.

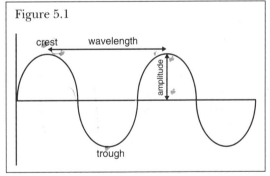

Figure 5.1

Problem

Radio Atlantic 252 broadcasts on 252 metres. If the velocity of radio waves in air is 3×10^8 m s^{-1} what is the frequency of the waves?

$$f = \frac{c}{\lambda} = \frac{3 \times 10^8}{252} = 0\cdot0119 \times 10^8 \text{ Hz} = 1190 \text{ kHz}$$

INTERFERENCE

If two trains arrived at the same point at the same time they would crash. On the other hand if you sit listening to a band playing music the sound waves from the different instruments do not crash. Instead they merge or combine. What happens when they combine is called interference.

Interference means that when two or more waves meet the resultant displacement is equal to the algebraic sum of the individual displacements.

Constructive interference occurs when two waves combine to give a wave of larger amplitude.

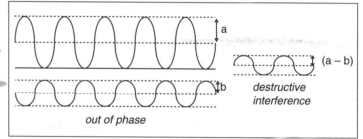

in phase

constructive interference

If the two waves are out of phase when they meet the result will be destructive interference.

Destructive interference occurs when two waves combine to give a wave of smaller amplitude.

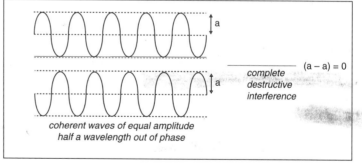

out of phase

destructive interference

The most interesting effect of all occurs when waves from coherent sources meet.

Coherent sources are sources that have the same frequency and are in phase with each other.

coherent waves of equal amplitude half a wavelength out of phase

complete destructive interference

$(a - a) = 0$

If coherent waves of equal amplitude have travelled different paths and the difference between their paths is half a wavelength, or an odd number of half wavelengths, then they will be half a wavelength out of phase and the result will be **complete destructive interference**. If the path difference is a whole number of wavelengths the waves will arrive in phase and the result will be constructive interference.

THE WAVE THEORY OF LIGHT

About 1680 a Dutchman called Christiaan Huygens said that light travelled from one place to another by means of a wave motion.

The wave theory was in conflict with the **corpuscular theory** put forward by Isaac Newton in 1660. The corpuscular theory says that light is composed of high-speed particles emitted by luminous bodies. According to this theory light would travel faster in a denser medium. According to the wave theory it would travel slower in a denser medium.

Also, if the wave theory were correct, it should be possible to get two light waves to meet and produce darkness (complete destructive interference). Two things happened which tilted the balance in favour of the wave theory:

1. A scientist called Foucault showed that light slowed down when it entered a denser medium.
2. In 1802 Thomas Young succeeded in producing interference patterns with light.

DIFFRACTION

If you are standing in the school corridor and two of your friends are talking loudly round the corner, you can hear what they are saying but you cannot see them. In other words sound waves travel round corners but light waves do not, at least not normally. In fact, light waves can also spread round corners in certain circumstances. The fact that waves can spread round corners can be demonstrated using a ripple tank as shown in Figure 5.2. In the first case some slight bending of the waves occurs but in the second case, when the width of the gap is about the same as the wavelength of the waves, the waves spread out round the corners of the obstacle.

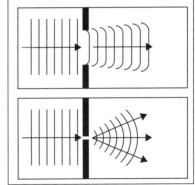

Figure 5.2

The spreading of waves into the geometric shadow of an obstacle is called diffraction.

It is not necessary to have a gap for diffraction to occur. If waves strike the edge of an object secondary waves can spread out from that edge so diffraction can occur at the edge of an object.

The longer the wavelength the greater the diffraction.

The diffraction grating

A diffraction grating consists of a large number of parallel lines ruled on a piece of transparent material. Light cannot pass through the lines but it can pass through the spaces between them. This means that the spaces act as a series of parallel slits. Diffraction occurs at each slit.

In general **$n\lambda = d \sin \theta$**

MANDATORY EXPERIMENT

AIM: TO MEASURE THE WAVELENGTH OF MONOCHROMATIC LIGHT USING A
DIFFRACTION GRATING.

Method

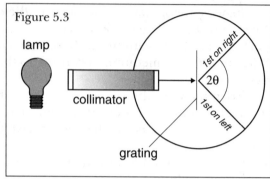

Figure 5.3

1. Adjust the spectrometer for parallel light.
2. Place the telescope in line with the collimator.
3. Clamp the grating on the table at right angles to the collimator.
4. Rotate the telescope to the left until the crosswires are on the first order image. Note the angle.
5. Repeat for the first order image on the right. The difference between the two readings gives 2θ.

The grating element d is indicated on the grating.

Result: λ can now be calculated from the formula $n\lambda = d \sin \theta$.

Problem 1

Monochromatic light falls normally on a diffraction grating having 500 lines per mm. If the second-order image occurs at an angle of $30°$ to the normal find the wavelength of the light.

5×10^2 lines per mm $= 5 \times 10^5$ lines per m

$$d = \frac{1}{(5 \times 10^5)} \text{ metres}$$

$2\lambda = d \sin \theta$

$$\lambda = \frac{d \sin \theta}{2} = \frac{(1 \times 0.5)}{(5 \times 10^5 \times 2)} = 0.5 \times 10^{-6} \text{ m} = 500 \times 10^{-9} \text{ m}$$

$= 500$ nanometers (nm)

Problem 2

If you were carrying out an experiment to measure the wavelength of monochromatic light using a spectrometer describe the step(s) you would take in each of the following cases:

(a) If the images seen in the telescope were very faint
(b) If the crosswires were unclear
(c) If the images on one side were above the centre of the eyepiece.

In using a spectrometer to measure the wavelength of sodium light with a diffraction grating which had 500 lines per mm, the following readings were noted for the positions of the images: 243° 30'; 217° 15'; 200°; 182° 45' and 163° 30'.

1. One of the angles was read wrongly. Which one was it? Give the reason for your answer.
2. Calculate the wavelength of the light used.

(a) Open the collimeter slit wider
(b) Focus the telescope
(c) Level the table.

1. 243° 30' is wrong because sin 43° 30' is not twice sin 17° 15'.
2. $d \sin \theta = n\lambda \Rightarrow \dfrac{(1 \times 0 \cdot 2965)}{(5 \times 10^{-5})} = 1\lambda \Rightarrow \lambda = 593$ nm

Radio and TV waves

Radio and TV waves can be diffracted. However, if you are listening to FM radio the VHF (very high frequency) waves have very short wavelengths and therefore do not diffract very well round hills. UHF (ultra-high frequency) waves that are used for TV have even shorter wavelengths and diffract even less. This can cause poor reception in valleys. Radio waves with long wavelengths diffract well.

POLARISATION

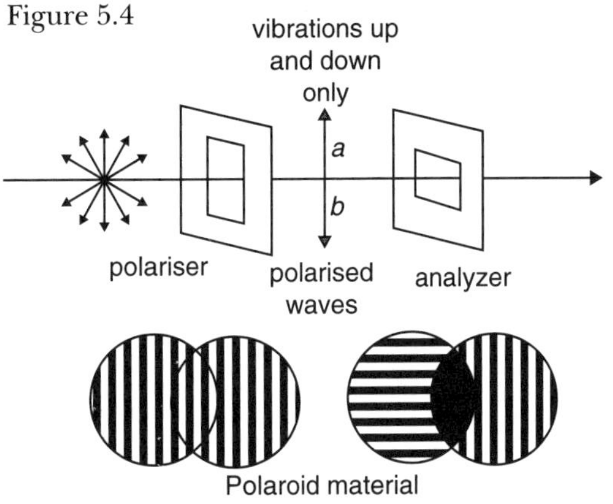

Light waves are transverse which means that they vibrate at right angles to the direction in which they are travelling. From Figure 5.4 we can see that the vibrations radiate out like a disc from the centre of the wave path. When the light meets the polariser only vibrations in the direction *ab* will pass through. The light has now been **polarised** which means that its vibrations are confined to one plane.

Figure 5.4

Radio and TV waves are polarised before being transmitted. This makes them less liable to interference but it is essential that your aerial is turned into the correct plane to receive them.

Only transverse waves can be polarised. The fact that light can be polarised shows that it is a transverse wave.

SUMMARY

- Transverse waves are waves that travel perpendicular to the direction of vibration of the particles.
- Longitudinal waves are waves that travel parallel to the direction of vibration of the particles.
- velocity = frequency × wavelength
- Interference means that when two or more waves meet, the resultant displacement is equal to the algebraic sum of the individual displacements.
- Constructive interference occurs when two waves combine to give a wave of larger amplitude.
- Destructive interference occurs when two waves meet to give a wave of smaller amplitude.
- Coherent sources are sources that have the same frequency and are in phase.
- The spreading of waves into the geometric shadow of an obstacle is called diffraction.
- The longer the wavelength the greater the diffraction.

Chapter 6 – The Spectrum

In 1660 Isaac Newton allowed a narrow beam of white light to strike a glass prism and found that the white light was split into seven colours, red, orange, yellow, green, blue, indigo and violet. The resultant band of colour is called a **spectrum** and the splitting of white light is called **dispersion**.

Dispersion is the splitting up of white light into its constituent colours.

The reason for dispersion is as follows: different-coloured lights have different wavelengths. As the light travels from one medium to another the long wavelengths are refracted least, the short wavelengths are refracted most and so the colours are separated slightly from each other.

PRIMARY COLOURS

Although white light can be split up into seven colours, white can be produced by mixing red, green and blue light in the proper proportions.

Red, green and blue are called primary colours.

All other colours are a combination of these and are called secondary colours.

Complementary colours are a primary colour and a secondary colour which together give white (e.g. blue and yellow).

DISPERSION BY A GRATING

When white light falls on a diffraction grating the different colours contained in white light are diffracted by different amounts. This means that the light is not only diffracted but also dispersed. Red light, which has the longest wavelength, is deviated most and violet (shortest wavelength) is deviated least. This is the exact opposite to the dispersion produced by a prism. Also, there is a lot of overlapping in the spectrum produced by the prism but not in the spectrum produced by the diffraction grating. Note that no spectrum is formed directly behind the grating because the path difference between all the waves here is zero.

Dispersion by diffraction: long wavelengths diffracted most.
Dispersion by refraction: long wavelengths refracted least.

THE ELECTROMAGNETIC SPECTRUM

In 1865 the Scottish physicist James Clerk Maxwell suggested a new theory of light. He said that light waves were really vibrating electric and magnetic fields. He also suggested that this **electromagnetic radiation** might exist at wavelengths greater than visible light and shorter than visible light. All electromagnetic waves are fundamentally the same but some have high frequencies and short wavelength (e.g. X-rays) while others have low frequencies and long wavelengths.

INFRA-RED

Infra-red radiation is given off by warm objects. Your body gives off infra-red rays. It is the infra-red radiation from the sun, a coal fire or an electric bar heater which heats you up. An electric light bulb gives out light and heat. We can see the light but not the infra-red rays (heat).

Applications of infra-red radiation

1. It has a heating effect and is used to help heal damaged muscles.
2. Using infra-red sensitive film doctors take photographs called **thermographs**.
3. Your remote control uses an infra-red beam to control your TV or video.
4. If there is a burglar alarm in your school it is probably designed to detect infra-red given out by an intruder.
5. Fire-fighters use infra-red viewers to search for unconscious people in smoke filled buildings or under rubble.

ULTRAVIOLET

Ultraviolet rays are given off by the sun and also by electric arcs used in electric welding. Small amounts of ultraviolet radiation are good for us, as they help our skin to produce vitamin D, but large amounts can cause sunburn or even skin cancer. Large amounts damage our eyes.

Fortunately for us, most of the sun's ultraviolet rays are absorbed by the **ozone layer** high in the atmosphere. Chlorofluorocarbons (CFCs) are damaging the ozone layer so that much more ultraviolet radiation is reaching the earth. CFCs have been banned in many countries.

Applications of ultraviolet radiation

1. Some substances **fluoresce** – they absorb ultraviolet rays and convert the energy to visible light rays. This is what happens in a fluorescent light tube.
2. Some washing powders contain chemicals (called brighteners) that fluoresce. This is why white clothes that have been washed in these powders appear so bright under the UV lamps in a disco.
3. Security pens contain special ink that you can use to write your name on your personal stereo, etc. This is invisible in ordinary light but it shows up clearly under UV light.

MICROWAVES

What we call microwaves are in fact radio waves of short wavelength. They have two main uses, communication and cooking.

1. Communication

Microwaves are not refracted much by the atmosphere, in fact they practically travel in straight lines. This means that microwaves can carry information on the Earth's surface from transmitter to receiver, but to do this transmitter and receiver must be in 'line of sight' of each other. Because of the curvature of the Earth's surface they must be, on average, within 40 miles of each other. However by using a series of transmitters and receivers signals can be sent right across the country.

For communication over longer distances microwaves can be sent from the surface of the Earth to satellites and back again.

2. Cooking

In a microwave oven the microwaves are produced by a magnetron and guided to a metal stirrer that reflects the waves into the oven. Microwaves are reflected by metal but absorbed by water, sugar and fat molecules in food. This causes the food to heat up and cook very rapidly. The door has a wire mesh to reflect microwaves back into the oven and a safety switch that turns off the microwave if the door is opened.

An emission spectrum is a spectrum given out by a substance when its atoms are excited.

There are a number of dark lines in the spectrum of the sun. This means that many wavelengths are missing because they were absorbed by gases in the sun's atmosphere. A German scientist, Joseph von Fraunhofer, measured the wavelengths of these lines that later became known as **Fraunhofer lines**. This type of spectrum is called an absorption spectrum.

An absorption spectrum is a spectrum that is continuous except for certain missing wavelengths.

LASERS

A laser tube produces a beam of light in which all the waves are of the same frequency and in phase. As a result of constructive interference a beam of high-energy light is produced. This narrow beam can be controlled with great precision.

Uses of the laser

Laser beams are used in eye surgery to treat a detached retina. The beam, which passes through the cornea and lens without damaging them, is focused on the retina and welds it in place.

The laser has replaced the scalpel in many cases. As it cuts through flesh the heat seals the cut blood vessels almost instantly so there is very little bleeding.

Computer controlled lasers can cut through up to 50 layers of cloth at a time with great speed and accuracy. Your jeans were probably cut out in this way. Lasers can also cut through steel.

A laser beam scans the underside of a compact disc converting the information stored there into electrical impulses that are later converted to sound.

Laser beams are also used at supermarket checkouts to scan bar codes etc.

SUMMARY

- Dispersion is the splitting up of white light into its constituent colours.
- The primary colours are red, green and blue.
- Complementary colours are a primary colour and a secondary colour that together give white.
- An emission spectrum is a spectrum given out by a substance when its atoms are in an excited state.
- An absorption spectrum is a spectrum that is continuous except for certain missing wavelengths.
- Fraunhofer lines are dark lines in the spectrum of the sun due to absorption.

Chapter 7 – Sound

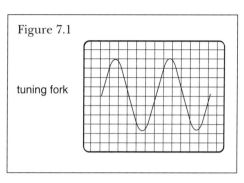

Figure 7.1

tuning fork

In order to produce sound something must vibrate.

THE WAVE NATURE OF SOUND

Connect a microphone to an oscilloscope. Strike a tuning fork to make it vibrate and hold it in front of the microphone. A **transverse** wave will appear on the screen with the same frequency as the **longitudinal** sound wave produced by the tuning fork as shown in Figure 7.1.

CHARACTERISTICS OF SOUND

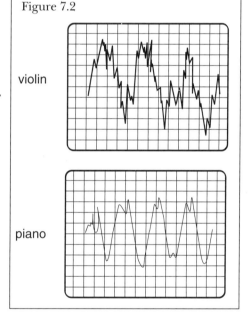

Figure 7.2

violin

piano

Sounds differ in three ways: (a) **pitch** (b) **loudness** (c) **quality** or **timbre**.

The pitch depends on the frequency.
The loudness depends on the amplitude.
The quality depends on the harmonics present.

A tuning fork produces a pure note that is a note of one frequency only. Notes produced by musical instruments, such as the piano and violin, consist of a basic frequency and a number of other frequencies which are multiples of the basic frequency. The lowest frequency is called the **fundamental frequency**. The other frequencies are called **harmonics.**

Harmonics are frequencies that are multiples of the fundamental frequency.

The fundamental frequency is sometimes called the **first harmonic** and all the other harmonics are called **overtones.**

The waveform you see on the screen and the sound you hear is produced by **interference** between the fundamental and the overtones. Different instruments produce different overtones and therefore different sounds.

The loudness of a note depends on the amplitude of the sound wave.

ULTRASONICS

Humans can hear sounds with frequencies between 20 Hz and 20 kHz. These are known as the **audio frequencies.** As we get older we become less sensitive to high frequencies. Sound waves with frequencies above 20 kHz are called **ultrasonics**. A dog whistle is a simple example of an ultrasound – it can be heard by dogs but not by humans.

Ultrasounds have many uses

1. *Sonar*
    This system can be used to find the depth of the sea. Sonar is also used by fishermen to detect shoals of fish. Ultrasound sonar systems are used to communicate with submarines travelling underwater.
2. *Ultrasound scanning*
    Ultrasound is beamed into the body. Echoes are produced as the sound meets different tissues such as bone, muscle, etc. These echoes can be used to build up an image on a screen of the stomach, a baby in the womb, etc. This system is much safer than X-rays.
    Waves can be used to break up painful kidney stones. The tiny pieces can then be passed out of the kidneys in the urine.

RESONANCE

Resonance is a transfer of energy between two bodies with the same natural frequency.

A pendulum has a natural frequency of vibration that depends on its length so it can be used to demonstrate resonance as shown in Figure 7.3. The heavy pendulum E is set in motion. This causes the others to vibrate but the one which vibrates most is B. This is because B and E have the same length and therefore the same natural frequency of vibration.

Resonance can cause problems

For example, much of the damage done by earthquakes is due to resonance between buildings or the ground under them, and the seismic waves from the earthquake. Resonance also occurs between the microwaves in a microwave oven and the food molecules.

Security tags in shops contain electronic circuits tuned to oscillate at a certain frequency. Radio transmitters at the doors send out waves of the same frequency. If anyone attempts to bring the tag out of the door resonance takes place and an alarm is set off.

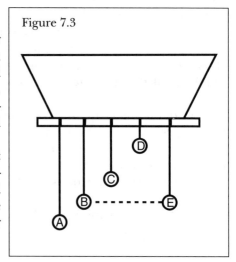

Figure 7.3

A stethoscope is used to listen to sounds from inside the body, in particular sounds from the heart and lungs. The doctor presses the open cone against the skin and uses the skin as a diaphragm. By varying the pressure of the cone on the skin the skin can be tuned to resonate with the heartbeat giving a louder sound.

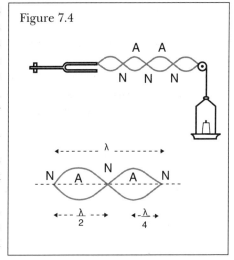

Figure 7.4

A stationary wave is produced when two waves of the same frequency and amplitude meet when moving in the opposite direction.

In Figure 7.4, as a result of interference a pattern of **stationary waves** or **standing waves** is formed. Certain points in the string are at rest and do not vibrate at all – these are called **nodes** (N). Other points vibrate with maximum amplitude – these are called **antinodes** (A).

The distance between successive nodes is half a wavelength.

The distance between a node and an antinode is quarter of a wavelength.

MANDATORY EXPERIMENT

AIM: TO MEASURE THE VELOCITY OF SOUND USING A RESONANCE TUBE.

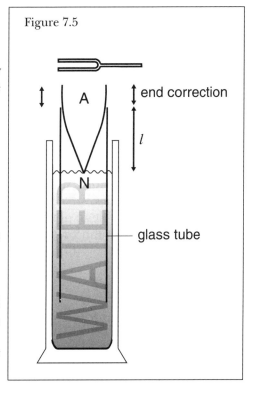

Figure 7.5

Method

1. Strike a tuning fork of known frequency and hold it over the air column in the tube.
2. Slowly raise the tube until the sound reaches a maximum. This is called the first position of resonance.
    (The antinode is not exactly at the top of the tube but a small distance, known as the end correction, above it.)
    Measure the distance l.
3. Take the end correction as being $0{\cdot}3$ times the diameter of the tube.
4. $\dfrac{\lambda}{4} = l + 0{\cdot}3d \Rightarrow \lambda = 4(l + 0{\cdot}3d)$
5. The velocity c can now be calculated from the formula $c = f\lambda$ where f is the frequency of the fork.

The velocity of sound in air is approximately 330 m s^{-1}.

VELOCITY OF SOUND IN OTHER MEDIA

The velocity of sound in a medium depends on the density and elasticity of the medium.

The velocity of sound in air is approximately 330 m s^{-1}. It is independent of the pressure but proportional to the square root of the absolute temperature. The velocity of sound in water is about 1,480 m s^{-1}. In iron it is about four times as great.

VIBRATIONS IN STRINGS

The music produced by guitars, violins and other string instruments are all examples of vibrations in strings.

The sonometer is used to study the vibrations of stretched strings. The length of string free to vibrate is varied by varying the distance between the bridges. The tension in the string is varied by varying the mass and therefore the weight at M, as shown in Figure 7.6.

MANDATORY EXPERIMENT

AIM: TO INVESTIGATE THE VARIATION OF THE FUNDAMENTAL FREQUENCY OF A STRING WITH LENGTH.

Method

1. Set the tension of the string at a convenient value and leave it fixed.
2. Strike a tuning fork of known frequency on a block of wood and place it in contact with bridge A.
3. Adjust B until the paper rider is thrown off the string. The string is now in resonance with the fork and will emit a note of the same frequency. Measure *l*.
4. Repeat this procedure with forks of different frequencies.
5. If you have been able to get 5 or more readings draw a graph of *f* against $\frac{1}{l}$. You should get a straight line through the origin.

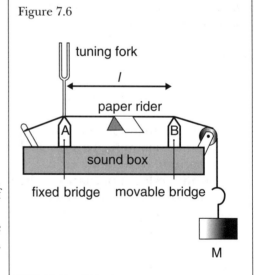

Figure 7.6

tuning fork

l

paper rider

A   B

sound box

fixed bridge   movable bridge

M

Conclusion: $f \propto \dfrac{1}{l}$.

The frequency of a stretched string is inversely proportional to its length.

MANDATORY EXPERIMENT

AIM: TO INVESTIGATE THE VARIATION OF THE FUNDAMENTAL FREQUENCY OF A STRING WITH TENSION.

Method

1. Set the length of the string at a convenient value and leave it fixed as in Figure 7.6.
2. Strike a tuning fork of known frequency on a block of wood and hold it in contact with the bridge A.
3. Adjust the tension (T) until the paper is thrown off the string. Note the tension.
4. Repeat this procedure with a number of forks of different frequency. Plot a graph of *f* against $\sqrt{T}$.

Result: A straight line through the origin.
Conclusion: $f \propto \sqrt{T}$.

The frequency of a stretched string is directly proportional to the square root of the tension.

If you look at the strings on a guitar you will see that the lowest frequency string is made of heavy material while the highest frequency string is made of light material. This would imply an inverse relationship between the mass of the string and the frequency. In fact the frequency is inversely proportional to the square root of the mass of unit length of the string.

$f \propto \dfrac{1}{\sqrt{\mu}}$ where μ is the mass of unit length of the string.

Putting all three factors together we find that in the case of the fundamental frequency

$$f = \frac{1}{2l}\sqrt{\left(\frac{T}{\mu}\right)}$$

Problem

A sonometer wire was tuned to a fundamental frequency of 250 Hz. The vibrating wire was then under a tension of 10 N and was 87 cm long. Calculate how to tune the wire to a fundamental frequency of 375 Hz by adjusting: (i) its length only, (ii) its tension only.

(i) $f \propto \dfrac{1}{l}$ If *f* is multiplied by $\dfrac{3}{2}$ then *l* is divided by $\dfrac{3}{2}$ · 0·87 divided by $\dfrac{3}{2}$ = 58 cm.

(ii) $f \propto \sqrt{T}$ If *f* is multiplied by $\dfrac{3}{2}$ then T is multiplied by $\dfrac{9}{4}$ · 10 × $\dfrac{9}{4}$ = 22·5N.

THE DOPPLER EFFECT

Have you ever noticed that as an ambulance approaches you the sound increases in pitch and as it goes away from you the sound decreases in pitch? This effect was predicted by Doppler in 1845. He said that when a source of sound waves (or light waves) was moving, a change in frequency should be observed.

The Doppler effect is the change in the frequency of waves due to relative motion between the waves and the observer.

The left-hand diagram in Figure 7.7 shows that source S is stationary. An observer at A and an observer at B receive waves of the same wavelength and the same frequency.

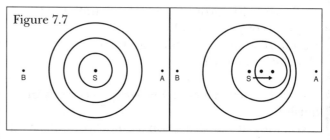

Figure 7.7

The right-hand diagram in Figure 7.7 shows that the source is moving toward A and away from B. The observer at A receives waves of reduced wavelength and **increased frequency.** The observer at B receives waves of increased wavelength and **reduced frequency.**

If c is the velocity of the waves, u is the velocity of the source, f is the frequency of the waves emitted by the source and f' the frequency of the waves received by the observer the formula for the Doppler effect is:

$$f' = \frac{fc}{(c \pm u)}$$

Problem

A train whistle emits a sound of frequency 500 Hz as the train approaches a station at a velocity of 40 m s^{-1}. Calculate the change in pitch of the sound as the train passes through the station.

(Velocity of sound in air = 340 m s^{-1}.)

(a) As the train approaches $f' = \dfrac{fc}{(c - u)} \Rightarrow f' = \dfrac{(500 \times 340)}{(340 - 40)} \Rightarrow f' = 566$ Hz.

(b) As the train leaves $f' = \dfrac{fc}{(c + u)} \Rightarrow f' = \dfrac{(500 \times 340)}{(340 + 40)} \Rightarrow f' = 450$ Hz.

Change in frequency = 566 − 450 = 116 Hz.

The Doppler effect is used by police in speed traps. It is used in air navigation and in tracking satellites. Scientists study the movement of stars by studying the light that comes from them. Photographs of the spectra of distant galaxies show that certain characteristic lines have shifted toward the red end of the spectrum. This **red shift** is caused by the Doppler effect and tells us that these galaxies are moving away from us rapidly.

SOUND INTENSITY

The term sound intensity is used to describe the amount of sound energy passing through a particular point.
Sound intensity is the energy per second passing through 1 square metre held at right angles to the direction in which the sound is travelling.

From this definition it follows that **the unit of sound intensity is the watt per metre squared (W m^{-2}).**

The threshold of hearing is the lowest intensity to which the human ear can respond when the frequency is 1 kHz.

A sound with an intensity of 10^{-12} W m^{-2} is known as the threshold of hearing because a sound of this intensity at a frequency of 1 kHz should just be audible to the average human ear. The intensity of any other sound **relative** to this threshold intensity can be expressed in units called **bels.**
  The bel (B) is the relative change in intensity between two sounds if the intensity of one is 10 times the intensity of the other.
  The bel is a very large unit so the **decibel (dB)** is used in practice. The range of sound intensities experienced by the human ear is so great that it takes a logarithmic scale to accommodate them. (The alternative would be to have numbers with 12 or more digits.)

Number of bels $= \log_{10} \dfrac{I_2}{I_1}$

Problem

When a student switches on her radio the sound intensity in her room increases from 10^{-8} W m^{-2} to 10^{-5} W m^{-2}. What is the relative increase in intensity?

Number of bels $= \log_{10} \dfrac{I_2}{I_1} = \log_{10} \dfrac{10^{-5}}{10^{-8}} = \log_{10} 10^3 = 3$ bels $= 30$ dB.

SOUND INTENSITY LEVEL

If we take 10^{-12} W m^{-2} as our basic unit and apply it to the above formula we get:
  Intensity level $= \log_{10} \dfrac{I}{10^{-12}}$ B or in decibels **$10 \left(\log_{10} \dfrac{I}{10^{-12}} \right)$ dB**

Problem

The sound intensity in heavy traffic is 8×10^{-5} W m^{-2}. What is the intensity level?

Intensity level $= \log_{10} \dfrac{(8 \times 10^{-5})}{10^{-12}} = \log_{10} (8 \times 10^7) = \log_{10} (8) + 7 = 7{\cdot}9$ B $= 79$ dB

SOUND WAVES AND LIGHT WAVES

Table 7.1

Light waves	Sound waves
electromagnetic, which means they are due to varying electric and magnetic fields	are due to vibrating particles
do not need a medium	need a medium
transverse	longitudinal
can be polarised	cannot be polarised
can be reflected, refracted and are subject to interference	can be reflected, refracted and are subject to interference
can be diffracted	sound waves diffract more due to their longer wavelength
travels in air at 3×10^8 m s^{-1}	sound travels in air at 330 m s^{-1}

SUMMARY

- The pitch of a note depends on the frequency.
- The loudness depends on the amplitude.
- Harmonics are frequencies that are multiples of the fundamental frequency.
- The quality of a note depends on the waveform (fundamental plus overtones).
- Resonance is the transfer of energy between two bodies of the same natural frequency.
- The Doppler effect is the change in the frequency of a wave due to relative motion between the source and the observer.
- Sound intensity is the energy per second flowing through one square metre held at right angles to the direction in which the sound is travelling.
- The unit of sound intensity is the watt per metre squared.
- The bel is the relative change in intensity between two sounds if the intensity of one is 10 times the intensity of the other.
- The threshold of hearing is the lowest intensity to which the human ear can respond when the frequency is 1 kHz.

Chapter 8 – Vectors and Scalars

Any quantity which has magnitude only is a Scalar.
Time, volume, mass etc. are scalars.

Any quantity which has both magnitude and direction is a Vector.
Velocity, force etc. are vectors.

The addition or subtraction of scalars is a simple matter, e.g. 3 seconds + 4 seconds = 7 seconds. However, in adding vectors so as to find their resultant, we must take direction into account, e.g. a man starting from A walks 3 km due east. He then walks 4 km due north. The resultant displacement from A is not 7 km but 5 km.
    N.B. Displacement is a vector having both distance and direction.

It is clear from the above examples that the addition of vectors is not quite as simple as the addition of scalars.

ADDITION OF VECTORS

We can find the resultant of two vectors by using the parallelogram law of vectors.
    Parallelogram Law of Vectors: If two vectors are represented by the two adjacent sides ab and ad of a parallelogram abcd, then the diagonal ac represents their resultant.

Problems in which these laws are used can be solved by accurate drawing or by calculation.

Problem 1

Find the resultant of a force of 3 units due north and a force of 4 units due east.
(a) By drawing.

Answer: A force of 5 units 37° north of east.

(b) By calculation.

$R^2 = 3^2 + 4^2 = 25 \Rightarrow R = 5$

$\tan \theta = \dfrac{3}{4} = 0 \cdot 75 \Rightarrow \theta = 36°52'$

Answer: A force of 5 units 36°52' north of east.

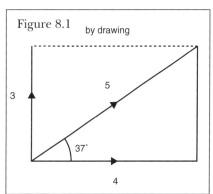

Figure 8.1 by drawing

3

5

37°

4

Problem 2

A parachutist is falling with a vertical velocity of 15 m s^{-1} when he is blown by a wind that has a horizontal velocity of 8 m s^{-1}. Calculate the resultant velocity of the parachutist. At a certain instant during the descent the parachutist is directly over a point X on the ground. The parachutist lands 10 seconds later at a point Y. What is the distance XY?

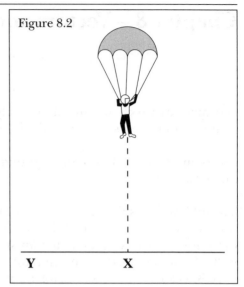
Figure 8.2

$R^2 = 15^2 + 8^2$ $\Rightarrow R^2 = 289$ $\Rightarrow R = 17$ m s^{-1}.
Angle = 28° to vertical.

Distance in any given direction
= velocity in that direction × time.
XY = 8 × 10 = 80 m.

RESOLUTION OF VECTORS

If two vectors can be replaced by a single vector, called their resultant, it is logical that the reverse is also true. So a vector can be **resolved** (split) into two components. The most convenient components of vectors are those at right angles to each other.

So vector R can be resolved into two components perpendicular to each other:
$R\cos \theta$ and $R\sin \theta$.

e.g. A force of 5 units acts in a direction 60° north of east. Its component due east is:

$5\cos 60 = 5(0\cdot5) = 2\cdot5$

A vector has no component in a direction at right angles to itself. For example if we consider a force of 10 units acting due east its component due north is $10\cos 90 = 10(0) = 0$.

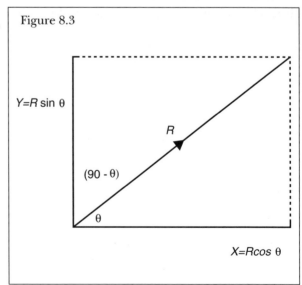
Figure 8.3

SUMMARY

- Any quantity which has both magnitude and direction is a vector.
- Any quantity which has magnitude only is a scalar.
- Parallelogram law: If two vectors are represented by two adjacent sides ab and ad of a parallelogram abcd then the diagonal ac represents their resultant.
- A vector has no component at right angles to itself.

Chapter 9 – Linear Motion

Displacement is the distance of a body from a fixed point in a particular direction.

A person starting at a point A and running due east at 6 m s^{-1} for 10 seconds, will undergo a displacement of 60 m due east.

The person might be thought to have had a velocity of 6 m s^{-1}. This statement is not true. The person had a speed of 6 m s^{-1} but a velocity of 6 m s^{-1} **due east**. In other words, speed is a scalar, velocity is a vector.

Velocity is speed in a given direction.
Velocity is the rate of change of displacement.

Acceleration is the rate of change of velocity.

Problem

A car takes 4 s to increase its velocity from 12 metres per second to 20 metres per second. What is the acceleration of the car?

Acceleration = change in velocity/time taken = $\dfrac{8 \text{ m s}^{-1}}{4 \text{ s}}$ = 2 m s^{-2}

A vector changes if either its magnitude or its direction changes. For example, a car that is going round a circular track at a steady rate of 60 km/h is constantly changing direction, so it is accelerating.

A body travelling at a constant speed has acceleration if it is changing direction.

In order to solve problems involving uniform acceleration, we need to derive three equations of motion. In these equations, we will use the following notation.

Notation: u = initial velocity, v = final velocity, a = acceleration, s = displacement, t = time
Change in velocity per second = acceleration

$$\frac{(v-u)}{t} = a \quad \Rightarrow \quad v - u = at$$
$$\Rightarrow \quad v = u + at \ (1)$$

Displacement = average velocity $\times$ time = $\dfrac{(u+v)}{2} \times t$

$$= \frac{(u+u+at)}{2} \times t$$

$$= (u + \frac{1}{2}at) \times t$$

$$s = ut + \frac{1}{2}at^2 \ (2)$$

From (1) $t = \dfrac{(v - u)}{a}$

Displacement = average velocity × time

$$s = \dfrac{(v + u)}{2} \times \dfrac{(v - u)}{a} \Rightarrow s = \dfrac{(v^2 - u^2)}{2a} \quad \Rightarrow v^2 - u^2 = 2as$$

$$\Rightarrow v^2 = u^2 + 2as \quad (3)$$

Care must be taken to use standard units with the above equations of motion.

Problem

A body accelerates uniformly from rest and travels 1,200 m in the first 30 seconds. Find the acceleration and the final velocity of the body.

$u = 0$, $s = 1{,}200$ m, $t = 30$ seconds, $v = ?$, $a = ?$

(1) $s = ut + \dfrac{1}{2} at^2 \Rightarrow 1{,}200 = 0 + \dfrac{1}{2} a(900) \Rightarrow 1{,}200 = 450a \Rightarrow \dfrac{8}{3} = a$

(2) $v = u + at \quad \Rightarrow v = 0 + \left(\dfrac{8}{3}\right)(30) \Rightarrow v = 80$

Answer: $8/3$ m s^{-2} and 80 m s^{-1}

Problem

A body starts from rest and accelerates at 5 m s^{-2} for 4 seconds. Its velocity remains constant for the next 10 seconds and it finally comes to rest with uniform retardation after a further 5 seconds. Find the total distance travelled.

Stage 1

$u = 0$, $v = ?$, $a = 5$ m s^{-2}, $t = 4$ s, $s = ?$

$s = ut + \dfrac{1}{2} at^2 \Rightarrow s = 0(4) + \dfrac{1}{2}(5)(16) \Rightarrow s = 0 + 40$

$s = \textbf{40 m}$

$v = u + at \quad \Rightarrow \quad v = 0 + (5)(4) \quad \Rightarrow \quad v = 20$ m s^{-1}

Stage 2

$v = 20$ m s^{-1} \qquad $t = 10$ s

distance = velocity × time = **200 m**

Stage 3

$u = 20$ m s^{-1}, $v = 0$, $a = ?$, $s = ?$, $t = 5$ s

$v = u + at \Rightarrow 0 = 20 + a(5) \quad \Rightarrow -20 = 5a \quad \Rightarrow -4 = a$

$v^2 = u^2 + 2as \quad \Rightarrow 0 = (20)^2 + 2(-4)s \quad \Rightarrow 0 = 400 - 8s \Rightarrow s = 50$ m

Total distance is $40 + 200 + 50 = 290$ m

VELOCITY-TIME GRAPHS

The velocity-time graph for the above example is shown in Figure 9.1. Note that:

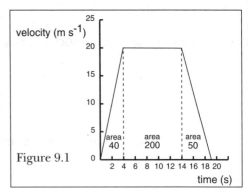

Figure 9.1

Velocity is given by the height of the graph.
Acceleration is given by the slope of the graph.
Distance travelled is given by the area under the graph.

Problem

The driver of a train travelling at 108 km/h sees another train 3 km ahead of him travelling at 90 km/h in the same direction on the same track. Find the least acceleration necessary to avoid a collision.

In this question we are dealing with relative motion so we can consider one train as being at rest and the other as approaching it at 18 km/h (i.e. 108 − 90). So in effect the train needs to reduce its velocity from 18 km/h to zero in a distance of 3 km or less (18 km/h = 5 m s^{-1}).

$$v^2 = u^2 + 2as \Rightarrow 0 = (5)^2 + 2a(3 \times 10^3) \Rightarrow 0 = 25 + 6a \times 10^3 \Rightarrow -25 = 6a \times 10^3$$
$$\Rightarrow -25/(6 \times 10^3) = a \Rightarrow a = -4 \cdot 166 \times 10^{-3} \text{ m s}^{-2}$$

ACCELERATION DUE TO GRAVITY

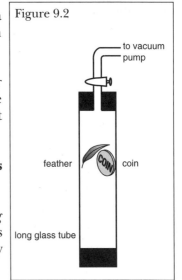

Figure 9.2

The air is first removed from the tube by means of a vacuum pump. The tube is then inverted and the coin and feather fall at the same speed.

If the air were not removed from the tube, the feather would fall more slowly than the coin, but this would be caused by air resistance not the difference in weight between the feather and the coin.

Ignoring air resistance the acceleration due to gravity is the same for all bodies at the same place.

A body falling freely experiences an acceleration g toward the centre of the earth. As this acceleration is uniform at a given place the equations of motion apply to it. The value of g is usually taken as 9·8 m s^{-2}.

    g always acts downwards.

If g is acting in the same direction as the velocity of a body then g is taken as positive. If it acts in the opposite direction to the velocity of the body g is taken as negative.

If a body is thrown vertically upwards with an initial velocity u, its velocity decreases by g units per second until it becomes zero.

A body at its highest point has zero velocity but not zero acceleration.
(Acceleration due to gravity still operates.)

MANDATORY EXPERIMENT

AIM: TO INVESTIGATE THE RELATIONSHIP BETWEEN PERIOD AND LENGTH FOR A SIMPLE PENDULUM (AND HENCE TO CALCULATE g).

Method

1. Attach the pendulum bob to one end of a light thread and clamp the other end of the thread between two pieces of cork.
2. Set the pendulum swinging through a small angle and take the time for 50 oscillations.
3. Find the periodic time T for one oscillation.
4. Carefully measure l, the distance from the cork to the centre of the pendulum bob.
5. Repeat for different values of l.
6. Plot a graph of T^2 against l. A straight line through the origin implies that $l \propto T^2$. The slope of this graph gives the value of $\dfrac{l}{T^2}$.

g can now be calculated from the formula $g = \dfrac{4\,\pi^2 l}{T^2}$

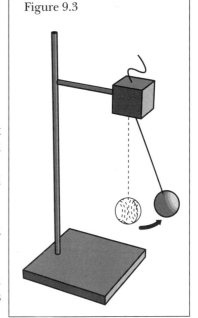

Figure 9.3

Note: We use a light thread so that practically all the mass is concentrated in the bob.

The pendulum formula is only valid for small angles.

MANDATORY EXPERIMENT

AIM: TO MEASURE g BY FREE FALL.

Method

1. With the switch K in position 1, the ball bearing is attached to the electromagnet with a small piece of paper between them.
2. When the switch is thrown to position 2 the ball bearing is released and the centisecond timer starts.

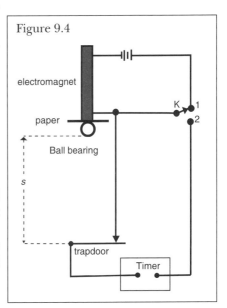

Figure 9.4

electromagnet

paper

Ball bearing

s

trapdoor

Timer

K
1
2

3. When the ball bearing hits the trapdoor the timer stops. The time for the free fall is now known.
4. Repeat a number of times and take the minimum time, t.
5. Measure s carefully. $s = ut + \frac{1}{2}at^2$.

In this case $u = 0$ so that $s = \frac{1}{2}gt^2$ $\Rightarrow$ $g = \frac{2s}{t^2}$

g can now be calculated.

Note: s should be at least 1 m.

SUMMARY

- Displacement is the distance of a body from a fixed point in a given direction.
- Velocity is speed in a given direction.
- Acceleration is rate of change of velocity.
- $v = u + at$, $s = ut + \frac{1}{2}at^2$, $v^2 = u^2 + 2as$

Chapter 10 – Forces

Force is anything that changes, or tends to change, the motion of a body in magnitude or direction.

Force is measured in newtons.

Look at the two objects in Figure 10.1. The first object will not move because the forces acting on it are balanced. The second object will move because the forces are unbalanced. **An unbalanced force causes motion.**

Weight

Every body on earth is acted on by a force that pulls it toward the centre of the earth.

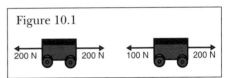

Figure 10.1

200 N   200 N   100 N   200 N

The force with which the earth attracts a body is called the weight of the body.

Since weight is a force it is measured in newtons.

Mass

Many people use the words 'weight' and 'mass' as if they meant the same thing – they don't.

The mass of a body is the amount of matter in it.
or
The mass of a body is its resistance to change of its existing motion. Mass is measured in kilograms.

MOMENTUM

Momentum is the product of the mass and the velocity of a body.
e.g. a body of mass 5 kg moving at 12 m s^{-1} has a momentum of 60 kg m s^{-1}.

NEWTON'S LAWS OF MOTION

1. A body remains at rest or moving with uniform velocity in a straight line unless an unbalanced force acts on it.
2. The rate of change of momentum is proportional to the force causing it and takes place in the direction of that force.
3. To every action there is an equal and opposite reaction. Action and reaction never act on the same body.

From Newton's second law: $F = ma$

$$\text{Force} = \text{mass} \times \text{acceleration}$$

This leads to the definition of the unit of force – the newton.

A newton is that force which gives an acceleration of 1 m s^{-2} to a mass of 1 kg.

Problem

A body leaves a point A and moves in a straight line with constant velocity 36 m s^{-1}. Seven seconds later another body of mass 2 kg at rest at A is acted on by a constant force of 4 N and moves in the same direction as the first body. How long will it take the second body to catch up with the first body?

For the second body $f = ma$ $4 = 2a$ $a = 2$ m s^{-2} $s = 1/2\, at^2 = t^2$.
For the first body $s = 36\,(t + 7) = 36t + 252$.
When they meet $t^2 = 36t + 252$ $t^2 - 36t - 252 = 0$ $(t - 42)(t + 6) = 0$ $t = 42$ s.

MANDATORY EXPERIMENT

AIM: TO SHOW THAT ACCELERATION IS PROPORTIONAL TO FORCE ($a \propto F$).

Method

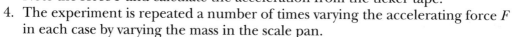

Figure 10.2

1. Set up the apparatus as shown in Figure 10.2.
2. Raise one end of the plank until, with a slight push, the trolley moves with constant speed.
3. Place a weight in the pan and let the trolley accelerate down the slope. Note the force F and calculate the acceleration from the ticker tape.
4. The experiment is repeated a number of times varying the accelerating force F in each case by varying the mass in the scale pan.
A graph of F against a gives a straight line through the origin showing that $a \propto F$.

Newton's second law underlines the difference between mass and weight. Since force = mass × acceleration, **weight = mass × g. On earth, weight = mass × 9.8.**

Impulse
Another way of looking at Newton's second law is as follows:

$$F = ma \implies F = m\frac{(v - u)}{t} \implies Ft = mv - mu.$$

Ft is known as the **impulse** so this formula can be stated in words as

Impulse = force × time = change in momentum.

This formula is useful for problems involving force and time.

Problem

A body of mass 5 kg moving at 2 m s^{-1} has its velocity increased to 6 m s^{-1} in 3 seconds under a constant force. Find the force.

$$Ft = mv - mu \quad \Rightarrow F \times 3 = 5 \times 6 - 5 \times 2 \quad \Rightarrow 3F = 20 \text{ N} \quad \Rightarrow F = \frac{20}{3} \text{ N}$$

APPLICATIONS

What would happen if you kicked a cement block as hard as you could? Right, you would probably break your toe – but why?

Let us assume that your foot has a mass of one kilogram and is travelling at 10 m s^{-1}. Suppose your foot is in contact with the block for one hundredth of a second.

$$Ft = mv - mu \quad \Rightarrow \quad F \times \frac{1}{100} = 1 \times 0 - 1 \times 10 \quad \Rightarrow \quad F \times \frac{1}{100} = 10 \quad \Rightarrow \quad F = 1,000 \text{ N}$$

The **shorter** the contact time the **greater** the force **and vice versa.**

Road safety

By designing a car so that the front crumples gradually on impact the collision time is increased and the force reduced. Serious injuries can also occur when a car is struck from the rear. For this reason modern cars are designed so that the front and rear both crumple gradually on impact but the cage (the part containing the passengers) is rigid.

Sport

When a tennis player is serving she can increase the contact time between the ball and the racket by following through. This increases the impulse and so increases the momentum.

Seat belts

According to Newton's first law a body remains at rest or moving with uniform velocity in a straight line unless an external force acts on it. If you are a passenger in a fast moving car which comes to a sudden stop you will continue moving with uniform velocity in a straight line out through the windscreen! A seat belt provides the external force that prevents this from happening. Seat belts are designed to stretch slightly to increase the collision time and so reduce the force of the belt on you.

Principle of conservation of momentum

If no external force acts on a system of colliding bodies, the total momentum of the bodies remains constant.

Mathematically $m_1 u_1 + m_2 u_2 = m_1 v_1 + m_2 v_2.$

Problem

A gun of mass 8 kg fires a bullet of mass 4 g with a velocity of 400 m s^{-1}. What is the velocity of recoil of the gun?

Total momentum before = total momentum afterwards.
$0 = 0.004 \times 400 + 8v \implies -8v = 1.6 \implies v = -0.2$ m s^{-1}
i.e. 0.2 m s^{-1} backwards.

JET PLANES AND ROCKETS

The principle of conservation of momentum and Newton's third law offer an explanation for the working of jet engines and rockets.

The hot gas rushes from the exhaust of the jet engine with great velocity. This causes the aeroplane to move forward. The rocket works in much the same way. The exhaust gas has a very high velocity and consequently a very large momentum. This gives the rocket an equal momentum in the opposite direction.

SPORT

If you were teeing off in a game of golf you would try to drive the ball as far as possible. To do this you would use a club called a driver. The head of a driver has a large mass which means that the momentum before impact is big. This means that the momentum after impact will also be big and the ball, of small mass, will travel a considerable distance.

MANDATORY EXPERIMENT

AIM: TO VERIFY THE PRINCIPLE
OF CONSERVATION OF
MOMENTUM.

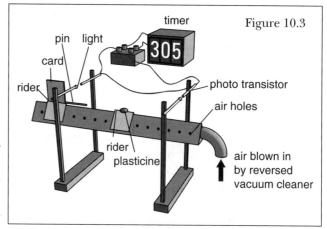

Figure 10.3

Method

1. Level the air track.
2. Find the mass of each complete rider.
3. Set up the apparatus as shown in Figure 10.3.
4. Give the first rider a slight push to set it in motion. As it passes the first photo transistor, the beam of light is interrupted and the transit time measured.
5. On impact the pin penetrates the plasticine and the two riders move along together. The new transit time is recorded as the card interrupts the beam of light striking the second photo transistor.

You should find that mass of first rider × velocity before impact = combined mass of riders × velocity after impact.

The air track with a single rider can be used to measure velocity.

MANDATORY EXPERIMENT

AIM: TO MEASURE THE VELOCITY OF A BODY.

Method

1. Give the rider a slight push in order to set it moving.
2. The transit time for the card gives the time it takes the rider to travel 0·1 m.
3. $\dfrac{\text{Distance}}{\text{time}}$ gives the velocity.

MANDATORY EXPERIMENT

AIM: TO MEASURE THE ACCELERATION OF A BODY.

Method

1. Place the photo transistors one metre apart for convenience.
2. Give the first rider a push in order to set it moving.
3. Note the transit time as it passes the first photo transistor. This is the time it takes to travel 0·1 m.
    $\dfrac{\text{Distance}}{\text{time}}$ gives the initial velocity u.
4. Repeat for the second photo transistor to get the final velocity v.
5. The distance s is 1 metre.
6. Calculate the acceleration from the formula $v^2 = u^2 + 2as$.

SUMMARY

*   A force is anything that changes, or tends to change, the motion of a body in magnitude or direction.
*   The force with which the earth attracts a body is called the weight of the body.
*   The mass of a body is the amount of matter in it.
*   Momentum is the product of the mass and the velocity of a body.
*   Force = mass × acceleration.
*   Weight = mass × g.
*   Principle of conservation of momentum: If no external force acts on a system of colliding bodies the total momentum of the bodies remains constant.

Chapter 11 – Moments

The point at which the whole weight of a body appears to act is called its centre of gravity.

STATES OF EQUILIBRIUM

The first flask shown in Figure 11.1 is in **stable** equilibrium, the second is in **unstable** equilibrium and the third is in **neutral** equilibrium.

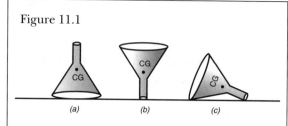

Figure 11.1

(a)   (b)   (c)

STABLE DESIGN

The principle of stable design is to have a **low centre of gravity and a wide base.**

LEVERS

A lever is a rigid body that is free to rotate about a fixed point, called a fulcrum.
    The turning effect of a force is called the **moment** of the force.

The moment of a force about a point is force × perpendicular distance from the point to the line of action of the force.

CONDITIONS FOR EQUILIBRIUM

Look at the metre stick in Figure 11.2.

Figure 11.2

0

10 N

20 N   50 N

Anti-clockwise moments		Clockwise moments
$(20 \times 20) + (10 \times 10)$	=	(50×10)
$400 + 100$	=	500
500 N m	=	500 N m

The metre stick is in equilibrium. The sum of the clockwise moments about O equals the sum of the anti-clockwise moments about O. This is an example of the principle of moments.

Principle of moments: When a body is in equilibrium the sum of the clockwise moments about any point is equal to the sum of the anti-clockwise moments about that point.

Another way of putting this is that the **vector** sum of the moments about any point is zero.

There are two conditions for equilibrium:
Condition 1: The principle of moments must apply.
Condition 2: The sum of the forces in any direction must equal the sum of the forces in the opposite direction.
   (Another way of saying this is that the **vector** sum of the forces in any direction is zero.)

Figure 11.3

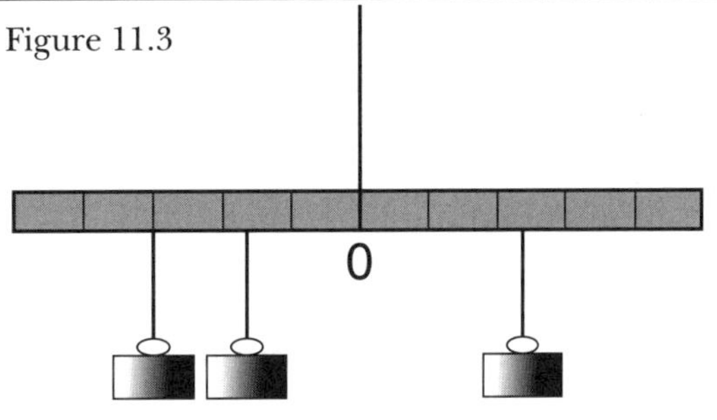

MANDATORY EXPERIMENT

AIM: TO INVESTIGATE THE LAWS OF EQUILIBRIUM FOR A SET OF COPLANAR FORCES.

0

Method
1. Find the mass of a metre stick and hang it from a stand.
2. Adjust the thread until the metre stick is balanced. The thread is now at the centre of gravity of the metre stick.
3. Hang a number of masses on the metre stick and adjust their positions until the metre stick balances.
4. Calculate the moments about O.
    Result: The sum of the clockwise moments equals the sum of the anti-clockwise moments.
5. Leaving the masses as they are, hang the metre stick from a suitable spring balance.
    Result: The reading on the spring balance equals the sum of all the weights including the weight of the metre stick (remember, weight = mass $\times$ g).
    Conclusion: The two laws of equilibrium have been obeyed.

Problem

Figure 11.4

The uniform metre stick in Figure 11.4 is in horizontal equilibrium. Find the weight of the metre stick and show how the principle of moments has been verified.

2·7 N   4·4 N

2·5 N   1·5 N   2·0 N

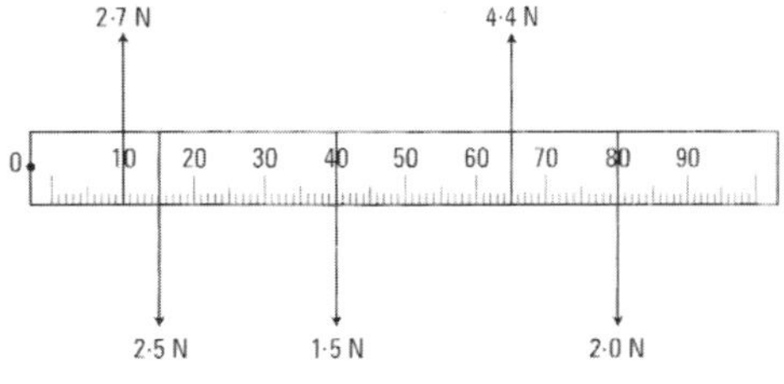

$2 \cdot 7 + 4 \cdot 4 = 2 \cdot 5 + 1 \cdot 5 + w + 2 \quad 7 \cdot 1 = 6 + w$
$w = 1 \cdot 1$ N
Taking moments about 0
$(2 \cdot 7 \times 10) + (4 \cdot 4 \times 65) = (2 \cdot 5 \times 15) + (1 \cdot 5 \times 40) + (1 \cdot 1 \times 50) + (2 \times 80)$

$313 = 313$

COUPLES

The moment of a couple is the product of one of the forces and the perpendicular distance between the two.

Couple $T = F \times d$

SUMMARY

- The point at which the whole weight of a body appears to act is called its centre of gravity.
- A lever is a rigid body that is free to rotate about a fixed point called the fulcrum.
- The moment of a force about a point is the force × the perpendicular distance from the point to the line of action of the force.
- The principle of moments states that when a body is in equilibrium the sum of the clockwise moments about any point is equal to the sum of the anti-clockwise moments about that point.
- The conditions for equilibrium are (a) the principle of moments must apply and (b) the vector sum of the forces in any direction is zero.
- The moment of a couple is the product of one of the forces and the perpendicular distance between the two.

Chapter 12 – Work, Energy and Power

Work = force multiplied by distance moved in the direction of the force.

$W = Fs$

A joule is the work done when a force of 1 newton moves its point of application 1 metre in the direction of the force.

ENERGY

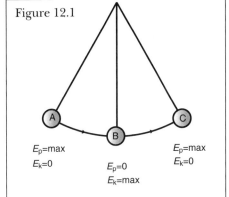

Figure 12.1

Energy is the ability to do work.
Potential energy is energy a body has due to its position or mechanical condition.
Potential energy (E_p) = mgh

Energy due to motion is called kinetic energy.
Kinetic energy (E_k) = $\frac{1}{2} mv^2$

1. When the pendulum is at its highest point A the potential energy is maximum, the kinetic energy is zero.
2. As the pendulum swings from A to B the potential energy changes completely to kinetic energy.
3. As it swings from B to C the kinetic energy changes back to potential energy.

The principle of conservation of energy states that energy can neither be created nor destroyed; it merely changes from one form to another.

When we do work we are changing energy from one form to another.

Problem 1

A body of mass 8 kg at rest on a smooth horizontal plane is acted on by a constant force for 0·5 minute. If the velocity of the body at the end of that time is 25 m s⁻¹ find (a) the force, (b) the distance travelled, (c) the work done on the body and (d) the final kinetic energy of the body.

(a) $u = 0$, $v = 25$ m s⁻¹, $t = 30$ s, a = ?
   $v = u + at$ $\Rightarrow 25 = 0 + a \times 30$ $\Rightarrow a = \frac{5}{6}$ m s⁻² $F = ma = 8 \times \frac{5}{6} = \frac{20}{3}$ N

(b) $s = ut + \frac{1}{2} at^2$ $\Rightarrow 0 + \frac{1}{2} \times \frac{5}{6} \times 900 = 375$ metres

(c) $W = Fs = \frac{20}{3} \times 375 = 2,500$ joules

(d) Since the body starts from rest its final kinetic energy is the work done on it which is 2,500 joules. Alternatively $E_k = \frac{1}{2} \, mv^2 = \frac{1}{2} \, (8) \, (25)^2 = 2{,}500$ joules.

Problem 2

A bullet of mass 20 g is fired into a block of wood of mass 380 g lying on a smooth table. The block moves off with a velocity of 10 m s^{-1}. Find the velocity of the bullet and the kinetic energy before and after the impact.

Momentum before = momentum after
$0 \cdot 02 \times v = (0 \cdot 02 + 0 \cdot 38) \times 10$
$0 \cdot 02 \times v = 0 \cdot 4 \times 10 \Rightarrow v = 200$ m s^{-1}

Total E_k before impact $= \frac{1}{2} \times 0 \cdot 02 \times 200^2 = 400$ J

Total Ek after impact $= \frac{1}{2} \times 0 \cdot 4 \times 10^2 = 20$ J

Note: Momentum is conserved but **kinetic** energy is not. 380 joules of energy is converted to heat and sound.

POWER

Power = $\dfrac{\text{work done}}{\text{time taken}}$ or **power is the amount of work done per second.**

Anything that does work is converting energy from one form to another. We can also say that power is the rate at which energy is converted from one form to another. Power is measured in watts: 1 watt = 1 joule s^{-1}.

Problem 1

A boy of mass 50 kg walks steadily up the stairs to the top of a building 40 m high. If the time taken is 2 minutes what is the power of the boy?

Force = mass × acceleration = 50 × 9·8 = 490 N
Work = force × distance = 490 × 40 = 19,600 J
Power = work done per second = $\dfrac{19{,}600}{120} = 163 \cdot 33$ watts

Problem 2

A pump raises 30 kg of water per minute to a height of 5 m and produces a muzzle velocity of 20 m s^{-1}. What is the power of the pump?

$E_p = mgh = 30 \times 9 \cdot 8 \times 5 = 1{,}470$ J
$E_k = \frac{1}{2} \times 30 \times 400 = 6{,}000$ J
$\dfrac{7{,}470}{60} = 124 \cdot 5$ W

Efficiency

The efficiency of a machine is a measure of how good it is at converting energy without waste. In science the efficiency of a machine is defined as follows:

$$\text{efficiency} = \frac{\text{power output}}{\text{power input}} \times 100\%$$

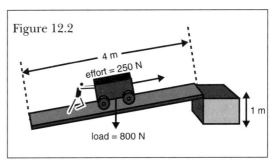

Figure 12.2

To understand how this operates consider one of the simplest machines of all, the **ramp** or **inclined plane**.

Suppose the man in Figure 12.2 pushes the load up the ramp and into the van in 20 seconds.

Useful work done = 800 N × 1 m = 800 J

Power output = $\frac{800\,\text{J}}{20\,\text{s}}$ = 40 W

Actual work done = 250 N × 4 m = 1,000 J

Power input = $\frac{1,000\,\text{J}}{20\,\text{s}}$ = 50 W

Efficiency = $\frac{(40 \times 100\%)}{50}$ = 80%.

The other 200 joules are lost as heat due to friction.

FRICTION

Friction is a force that opposes relative motion between two bodies in contact.

Friction always opposes motion. **Lubricants are substances that reduce friction.**

Static and dynamic equilibrium

In an earlier chapter we saw that a metre stick could be in equilibrium under the action of a number of coplanar forces. Since the metre stick is not moving it is in **static equilibrium.**

When a car is travelling at constant speed the forces acting on it are balanced. In other words, the force provided by the engine is balanced by friction between the road and the tyres and air resistance. Since the car is moving this is a case of **dynamic equilibrium.**

VISCOSITY

Viscosity is resistance to flow in fluids.

A sphere falling through a fluid has three forces acting on it:

1. its weight W acting downwards
2. an upthrust U due to displaced fluid (Archimedes)
3. a frictional force F acting upwards.

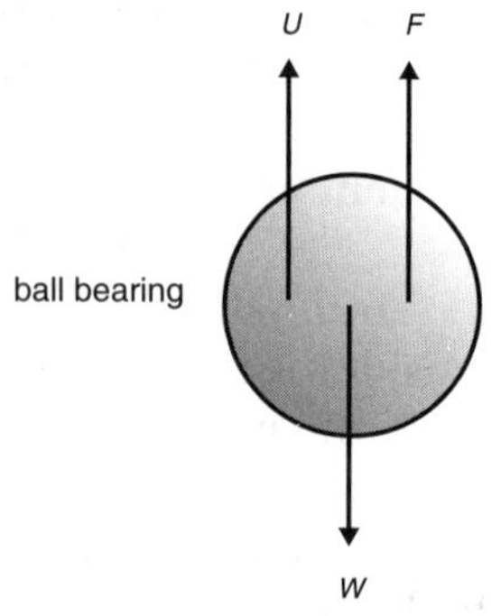

W and U are constant, but F increases with velocity. So as the sphere begins to fall, it accelerates. But as its velocity increases F increases until a stage is reached where $U + F = W$. At this stage the net force on the sphere is zero. According to Newton's first law the sphere will now continue to fall with a uniform velocity known as its terminal velocity.

Figure 12.3

SUMMARY

- Work = force × distance moved in the direction of the force.
- A joule is the work done when a force of one newton moves its point of application one metre.
- Potential energy is energy a body has due to its position or mechanical condition.
- Kinetic energy is energy due to motion.
- Power is the amount of work done per second.
- 1 watt = 1 joule s^{-1}
- Friction is a force that opposes relative motion between two bodies in contact.
- Viscosity is resistance to flow in fluids.

Chapter 13 – Density and Pressure

The mass of unit volume of a substance is called its density.

If a piece of iron of mass 39 g has a volume of 5 cm^3, what is its density?
The mass of 5 cm^3 = 39g
$\Rightarrow$ the mass of 1 cm^3 = $\dfrac{39 \text{ g}}{5 \text{ cm}^3}$
$\Rightarrow$ the density of iron is 7·8 g cm^{-3}

Density = mass/volume.

Mathematically $\rho = m/V$ where ρ is the density and V is the volume.
　The SI unit of density is kg m^{-3}, but g cm^{-3} is more convenient.

FLOATING AND DENSITY

A body will float in a fluid if it is less dense than the fluid.

PRESSURE

Pressure = $\dfrac{\text{force}}{\text{area}}$ or Pressure is force per unit area.

The weight of the block in Figure 13.1 is 600 N. The base area is 3 cm $\times$ 4 cm = 12 cm^2.
　The pressure = $\dfrac{\text{force}}{\text{area}}$ = $\dfrac{600 \text{ N}}{12 \text{ cm}^2}$ = 50 N cm^{-2}.

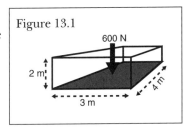

Figure 13.1

ATMOSPHERIC PRESSURE

We live at the bottom of a sea of air called the earth's atmosphere. The air, like everything else, has weight. Since it has weight it exerts pressure. Standard atmospheric pressure is = 1·013 $\times$ 10^5 N m^{-2}.

1 pascal (Pa) = 1 N m^{-2}

The atmospheric pressure now becomes 1·013 $\times$ 10^5 pascal or, more commonly, **1013 hectopascals**. High atmospheric pressure generally indicates dry weather, low pressure indicates wet weather.

PRESSURE IN FLUIDS

In fluids pressure depends on depth, density and the acceleration due to gravity.
Mathematically $P = h\rho g$.

Problem

In Figure 13.2 the area of piston A is 25 cm² and the area of piston B is 2,000 cm².
A 5 kg mass is placed on A.

(i) What is the downward force on A?
(ii) What is the pressure on the oil under A?
(iii) What is the pressure on the oil under B?
(iv) What is the upward force on B?

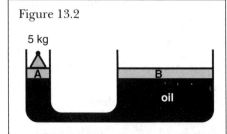

Figure 13.2

(i) Force = $5 \times 9\cdot8 = 49$ N
(ii) $\dfrac{49}{25} = 1\cdot96$ N cm²
(iii) $1\cdot96$ N cm²
(iv) $1\cdot96 \times 2,000 = 3,920$ N.

ARCHIMEDES' PRINCIPLE

Archimedes Principle: A body wholly or partially immersed in a fluid experiences an upthrust equal in magnitude to the weight of the fluid displaced.

Another way of saying this would be:
When a body is partly, or wholly immersed in a fluid, the apparent loss in weight equals the weight of the fluid displaced.

A floating body displaces its own weight of fluid.

SUMMARY

• The mass of unit volume of a substance is called its density.
• Pressure is force per unit area.
• The unit of pressure is the pascal. (1 pascal = 1 N m⁻²)
• Pressure in a liquid depends on depth and density.
• Archimedes Principle: A body partly or wholly immersed in a fluid experiences an upthrust equal to the weight of the fluid displaced.
• Law of Flotation: A floating body displaces its own weight of fluid.

Chapter 14 – Circular Motion

When a body is in uniform circular motion the Periodic Time (T) is the time for one complete revolution.

The velocity can be viewed in two ways. We can consider the angle being swept out in one second. This is called the **angular velocity (ω)**.

The angular velocity is the rate of change of angle measured in radians per second. $\omega = \frac{\theta}{t}$

$T = \frac{2\pi}{\omega}$

linear velocity $v = r\omega$

Problem

A particle is travelling at a constant speed round a circle of radius 20 cm. If the particle does 5 revolutions per second, find its angular and linear speed.

$\omega = 2\pi \times 5 = 10\pi = 31 \cdot 4 \text{ rad s}^{-1}$
$v = r\omega = 0 \cdot 2 \times 31 \cdot 4 = 6 \cdot 28 \text{ m s}^{-1}$

CENTRIPETAL FORCE

A body is kept moving in a circle by a force, called the centripetal force, acting toward the centre of the circle.

The centripetal force required depends on:

1. the mass of the body
2. the speed of the body
3. inversely on the radius of the circle.

FORCE AND ACCELERATION

If a body is in uniform circular motion its velocity is constant in magnitude **but not in direction**. So it has an acceleration.

Acceleration toward the centre of the circle is $a = r\omega^2$ or, $a = \frac{v^2}{r}$.

The force F necessary to keep a body of mass m moving in a circle is therefore $F = \frac{mv^2}{r}$ or $mr\omega^2$.

Problem

An electron of mass 9×10^{-31} kg circles the nucleus of an atom with a linear velocity of 3×10^6 m s^{-1}. The radius of its circular path is 6×10^{-10} m. Find the acceleration toward the centre and the centripetal force.

$$a = \frac{v^2}{r} = \frac{(3 \times 10^6)^2}{(6 \times 10^{-10})} = \frac{(9 \times 10^{12})}{(6 \times 10^{-10})} = 1{\cdot}5 \times 10^{22} \text{ m s}^{-2}$$
$$F = \frac{mv^2}{r} = 9 \times 10^{-31} \times 1{\cdot}5 \times 10^{22} = 1{\cdot}35 \times 10^{-8} \text{ N}$$

PLANETARY MOTION

In 1609 Kepler published his laws of planetary motion.

1. The planets move in elliptical orbits round the sun as one focus.
2. The line joining the sun and the planets sweeps out equal areas in equal time intervals.
3. The square of the periodic time of a planet is proportional to the cube of its mean distance from the sun.

GRAVITATION

Gravitation is the attraction that all masses in the universe have for each other. In 1680 Newton published his law of gravitation.

Law of gravitation: The force of attraction between any two bodies is proportional to the product of their masses and inversely proportional to the square of the distance between them.

$$F \propto \frac{(m_1 \times m_2)}{d^2} \quad \Rightarrow \quad F = \frac{Gm_1m_2}{d^2}$$

G is called the **constant of universal gravitation**

$$G = 6{\cdot}67 \times 10^{-11} \text{ N m}^2 \text{ kg}^{-2} \qquad \frac{g}{G} = \frac{M}{r^2}$$

DIFFERENT PLANETS

G has the same value everywhere in the universe. g is the acceleration due to gravity on any particular planet. Different planets have different masses and different radii. It follows that the acceleration due to gravity g varies from one planet to another.

$$\Rightarrow \frac{g_1}{g_2} = \frac{M_1 r_2^{\,2}}{M_2 r_1^{\,2}}$$

Problem

Given that the acceleration due to gravity on the earth is 9·8 m s^{-2}, find the acceleration due to gravity on the moon if the mass of the moon is one eightieth that of the earth and the radius of the moon is one quarter that of the earth.

$$\frac{g_{m}}{g_{e}} = \frac{M_{m}r_{e}^{2}}{M_{e}r_{m}^{2}} \Rightarrow \frac{g_{m}}{9·8} = \frac{1}{80} \times \frac{16}{1} = \frac{1}{5} \Rightarrow g_{m} = \frac{9·8}{5} = 1·96 \text{ m s}^{-2}$$

SATELLITES IN ORBIT

One of the greatest advances in the field of communications has been the use of communication satellites. Basically what happens is that a signal is transmitted from the earth's surface to a satellite and from there to somewhere else on the earth's surface. For this to succeed the satellite must always be directly above a particular point on the earth's surface. In other words the period of the satellite must be the same as the period of rotation of the earth, i.e. 24 hours. Such a satellite is said to be in a **geostationary** or **parking orbit**.

Problem

Given that the mass of the earth is 6×10^{24} kg and that the radius of the earth is $6·4 \times 10^{6}$ m, calculate the height above the earth's surface of a satellite that is in a geostationary orbit.

According to Kepler's third law:

$$\frac{4\pi^{2}r^{3}}{GM} = T^{2} \Rightarrow r^{3} = \frac{GMT^{2}}{4\pi^{2}} = \frac{6·67 \times 10^{-11} \times 6 \times 10^{24} \times (24 \times 3600)^{2}}{(4 \times 3·14)^{2}}$$

$$= 7·575 \times 10^{22} \text{ m} \Rightarrow r = 4·231 \times 10^{7} \text{ m}$$

The height above the earth's surface is the radius of the satellite's orbit minus the radius of the earth.

$$h = 4·231 \times 10^{7} - 6·4 \times 10^{6} = 3·591 \times 10^{7} \text{ m}$$

STRETCHING MATERIALS

Over three hundred years ago Robert Hooke did a series of experiments to see how the extension of a material and the stretching force were related.

The ability of the spring to return to its original shape is called **elasticity**.

If the spring is stretched too far it cannot return to its original shape. In this case it has been stretched beyond its **elastic limit.** Hooke summarised what he had learned in a law known as Hooke's law.

Provided the spring is not extended beyond its elastic limit the extension is proportional to the load.

Hooke's law applies to car springs, bed springs and steel girders. Graphs of extension against load are studied by construction engineers. The fact that the extension is proportional to the load allows the spiral spring to be used as a spring balance.

SIMPLE HARMONIC MOTION

The motion of a body is simple harmonic motion if its acceleration toward a particular point is directly proportional to its displacement from that point.

$a = -\omega^2 s$. **This is a mathematical definition of simple harmonic motion.**

The minus indicates that the body begins to retard as it passes through O, the centre of its motion.

SUMMARY

- For a body in circular motion: the periodic time T is the time for one complete revolution.
- The angular velocity is the rate of change of angle measured in radians per second.
- $T = \dfrac{2\pi}{\omega}$
- $\omega = \dfrac{\theta}{t}$
- $v = r\omega$
- Acceleration $= r\omega^2$ or $\dfrac{v^2}{r}$
- $F = \dfrac{mv^2}{r}$ or $mr\omega^2$
- A body is kept in circular motion by a force, called the centripetal force, acting toward the centre of the circle.
- Law of gravitation: The force of attraction between any two bodies is proportional to the product of their masses and inversely proportional to the square of the distance between them.
- $F = \dfrac{Gm_1 m_2}{d^2}$
- The motion of a body is simple harmonic motion if its acceleration toward a particular point is proportional to its displacement from that point. Mathematically $a = -\omega^2 s$

     When a particle is undergoing simple harmonic motion its acceleration is a maximum when its displacement is a maximum.

Chapter 15 – Heat, Temperature and Thermometers

THE THERMOSTAT

A thermostat is a device that is used to maintain a steady temperature in a room, an oven, a boiler, etc.

The two liquids commonly used in thermometers, mercury and alcohol, are compared in the following table:

Table 15.1

Mercury	Alcohol
1. Measures from −39 to 357°C	1. Measures from −112 to 78°C
2. Takes in little heat	2. Takes in more heat than mercury
3. Easily seen	3. Must be coloured
4. Does not stick to the glass	4. Sticks to the glass
5. Expands less than alcohol	5. Expands more than mercury

The use of water in thermometers was rejected because water does not expand evenly, it sticks to the glass, is a poor conductor, boils at 100°C and freezes at 0°C.

Temperature indicates the level of heat (hotness) in a body, not the amount of heat.

A thermometric property is a property that changes measurably as the temperature changes.

In addition to a substance with a thermometric property a good thermometer should have the following properties:

1. Accuracy
2. A wide range
3. Sensitivity
4. Quick to reach thermal equilibrium
5. Low heat capacity (it should take only a little heat from the body whose temperature it is measuring).

THE THERMOCOUPLE

If two wires made of different metals are joined together and the junction is heated an emf (voltage) is generated and a current flows. Since the emf changes as the temperature changes it can be used as a thermometric property. This type of thermometer is called a thermocouple.

MANDATORY EXPERIMENT

AIM: TO DRAW THE CALIBRATION CURVE OF A THERMOMETER USING A MERCURY THERMOMETER AS STANDARD.

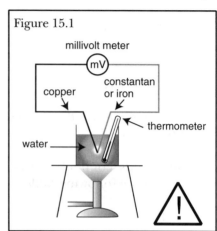

Figure 15.1

Method

1. Set up the apparatus as shown in Figure 15.1. Read the temperature and the voltage.
2. Raise the temperature of the water by 10°C. Read the temperature and the voltage.
3. Repeat the procedure until you have at least 5 readings. Plot a graph of temperature against voltage.

OTHER THERMOMETERS

Thermometers based on different thermometric properties do not agree with each other except at the ice point and the steam point. The reason for this is that the change in length of a column of mercury caused by a change in temperature of 1°C may not correspond with the change in pressure of a gas at constant volume, or the change in resistance of a piece of wire or the change in emf of a thermocouple. This does not mean that any of these thermometers is giving the wrong temperature. Each is giving the correct temperature as defined by its own particular thermometric property.

Boyle's law: At constant temperature the pressure of a fixed mass of gas is inversely proportional to its volume (pV is constant).

MANDATORY EXPERIMENT

AIM: TO VERIFY BOYLE'S LAW.

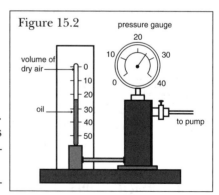

Figure 15.2

Method

1. Set up the apparatus as shown in Figure 15.2.
2. Open the tap and pump up the oil as far as possible or until the gauge reaches its maximum reading. Close the tap.
3. Wait a few minutes before reading the pressure and the volume.
4. Open the tap slightly until the pressure falls to a convenient reading. Close the tap, wait a few minutes and read the new pressure and volume.
5. Repeat this about 7 times and plot a graph of p against $\frac{1}{V}$.

The result should be a straight line through the origin.

If no pump is connected and the tap is open, the gauge will read atmospheric pressure.

An ideal gas is a gas that obeys Boyle's law exactly at all temperatures and pressures. In fact there is no such gas, but the behaviour of real gases at low pressure approaches the behaviour of an ideal gas.

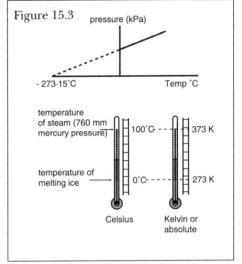

Figure 15.3

Absolute zero of temperature is −273·15°C.

Another scale of temperature is the **absolute scale** or **Kelvin scale.**
On this scale the thermometric property is pV for an ideal gas.

$0°C = 273·15$ K $−273·15°C = 0$ K. This last temperature is known as absolute zero. For all but the most accurate work **absolute zero** is taken as −273°C.

SUMMARY

- Heat is a form of energy.
- Temperature is a measure of how hot a body is.
- A thermometric property is a property that changes measurably with temperature.
- Boyle's law: At constant temperature the pressure of a fixed mass of gas is inversely proportional to its volume. pV is constant.
- An ideal gas is a gas that obeys Boyle's law exactly. Many gases approach the ideal at successively lower pressures.
- −273·15°C is known as absolute zero.

Chapter 16 – Transmission of Heat

Conduction is the way in which heat travels through a substance from one particle to the next (but the particles themselves do not travel).

Convection means that heat is carried through liquids and gases by the movement of heated particles.

Heat radiation is the transfer of energy by means of electromagnetic waves.

Dark surfaces are better than bright surfaces at radiating and absorbing heat.

The solar constant is the average energy per second falling normally on 1 m^2 of the earth's atmosphere.
(The value is $1{\cdot}4 \times 10^3$ W m^{-2}.)

The amount of this energy that actually reaches any point on the earth's surface depends on the weather conditions at that point.

The U-value is a measure of the heat lost per second through each square metre for each 1°C difference in temperature between the inside and the outside.

The unit of U-value is the watt per metre squared per kelvin (W m^{-2} K^{-1}).

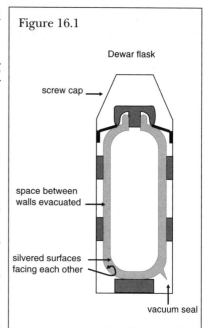

Figure 16.1

Dewar flask

screw cap →

space between
walls evacuated →

silvered surfaces
facing each other →

vacuum seal

This flask is designed to prevent heat travelling through its walls by conduction, convection or radiation.

Problem

Explain the basic physical principles involved in each of the following:

(a) A thermos flask can be used to keep ice from melting.
(b) On a cold day the bare metal handlebars of a bicycle feel colder than the plastic handgrips.
(c) Putting a meshed metal fireguard in front of a fire reduces the amount of heat reaching the room.
(d) People wear white clothes in both hot and cold climates.

(a) Heat cannot travel through the walls out or in so the heat needed to melt the ice cannot get in.
(b) The plastic acts as an insulator to prevent heat from flowing out of your hand so you feel less cold.
(c) The air trapped in the mesh acts as an insulator.
(d) Light surfaces are poorer absorbers and poorer radiators of heat.

SUMMARY

- Conduction is the way in which heat travels through a substance from one particle to the next (but the particles themselves do not travel).
- Convection is the way in which heat is carried through a fluid by the movement of heated particles.
- Heat radiation is the transfer of energy by means of electromagnetic waves.
- Dark surfaces are better than bright surfaces at radiating and absorbing heat.
- The solar constant is the average energy per second falling normally on 1 m^2 of the earth's atmosphere. The value is $1 \cdot 4 \times 10^3$ W m^{-2}.
- The U-value is a measure of the heat lost per second through each square metre for every 1 K difference in temperature between the inside and the outside. The unit of U-value is the W m^{-2} K^{-1}.
- Insulation reduces the U-value.

Chapter 17 – Heat Capacity and Latent Heat

The heat capacity of a body is the amount of heat required to raise the temperature of the body by 1 K.

The amount of heat required to raise the temperature of 1 kg of a substance by 1 K is called its specific heat capacity.

The amount of heat gained or lost = mass × specific heat capacity × change of temperature.

$Q = m \cdot c \cdot \Delta\theta$ **where Q is the heat energy, m is the mass of the body, c is the specific heat capacity, $\Delta\theta$ is the change in temperature.**

Problem

How much heat is required to raise the temperature of 10 kg of water from 20°C to 50°C?

$10 \times 4200 \times 30 = 1{,}260{,}000 \, \text{J} = 1{,}260 \, \text{kJ}$

MANDATORY EXPERIMENT

AIM: TO FIND THE SPECIFIC HEAT CAPACITY OF A METAL.

Method

1. Find the mass of the block of metal.
2. Set up the apparatus as shown in Figure 17.1.
3. Read the initial temperature on the thermometer and zero the joulemeter.
4. Allow current to flow until a temperature rise of at least 5°C has been achieved.
5. Wait a few minutes for the heat to spread throughout the metal block before taking the final temperature.

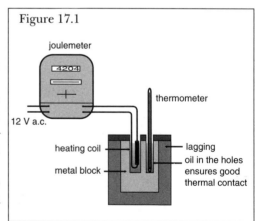

Figure 17.1

joulemeter

4204

+

12 V a.c.

thermometer

heating coil

metal block

lagging

oil in the holes ensures good thermal contact

Reading on joulemeter = mass × SHC × rise in temperature of block. SHC (specific heat capacity) is the only unknown.

9⚡5

Problem

The following is a typical set of readings: Mass of aluminium block 500 g, initial temperature 12°C, final joulemeter reading 4,204 J, final temperature 21·5°C. Find the specific heat capacity of the metal.

Energy supplied = Heat gained by aluminium
4,204 = 0·5 × *c* × 9·5
c = 885 J kg^{-1} K^{-1}

MANDATORY EXPERIMENT

AIM: TO FIND THE SPECIFIC HEAT CAPACITY OF A LIQUID.

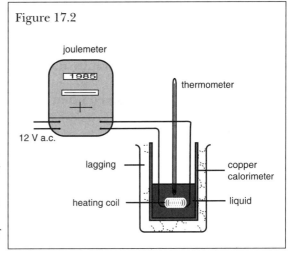

Figure 17.2

Method

1. Find the mass of the calorimeter.
2. Find the mass of the calorimeter plus the liquid.
3. Set up the apparatus as shown in Figure 17.2.
4. Note the initial temperature of the liquid.
5. Zero the joulemeter and allow current to flow until a temperature rise of at least 5°C has been achieved.
6. Note the final temperature and the final joulemeter reading.
7. The specific heat capacity can be calculated from the following equation:

Heat supplied = heat gained by calorimeter + heat gained by liquid. SHC of liquid is the only unknown.

Using a larger mass of liquid while supplying the same amount of energy would result in a smaller rise in temperature and possibly a larger percentage error.

Problem 1

The temperature of the water at the bottom of a waterfall is 1°C higher than the temperature at the top. Find the height of the waterfall. Specific heat capacity of water is 4,200 J kg^{-1} K^{-1})

Potential energy of the water at the top is *mgh* joules.
Heat gained by the water in falling is $m \times 4{,}200 \times 1$ joules.

$$\Rightarrow m \times 9{\cdot}8 \times h = m \times 4{,}200 \times 1$$

$$\Rightarrow h = \frac{4{,}200}{9{\cdot}8} = 428{\cdot}5 \text{ metres}$$

Problem 2

A 300 watt electric drill is used to drill a hole in an iron bar of mass 1 kg. If 80% of the energy used appears in the iron as heat, calculate the rise in temperature of the iron in 20 seconds. (Specific heat capacity of iron is 460 J kg^{-1} K^{-1}.)

300 watts = 300 joules per second $\Rightarrow$ 6,000 joules in 20 seconds
80% = 4,800 joules
heat gained by the bar = $1 \times 460 \times \theta = 4,800$
$\Rightarrow \theta = \dfrac{4,800}{460} = 10 \cdot 4$ K

There is no change of temperature during a change in state.

Latent heat is the heat involved when a substance changes state without changing temperature.

Heat energy needed to change state: $Q = ml$
where Q is the heat energy, m is the mass of the body, l is the specific latent heat.

The specific latent heat of fusion of ice is the amount of heat needed to change 1 kg of ice to water without a change of temperature.

The specific latent heat of vaporisation of water is the amount of heat needed to change 1 kg of water to steam without a change of temperature.

MANDATORY EXPERIMENT

AIM: TO FIND THE SPECIFIC LATENT HEAT OF FUSION OF ICE.

Method

1. Place some small lumps of ice in water and keep taking the temperature until it reaches 0°C.
2. In the meantime find the mass of a calorimeter.
3. Add some slightly warmed water to the calorimeter and find the mass of the calorimeter plus water.
4. Lag the calorimeter as shown in Figure 17.3 and take the initial temperature.
5. Dry the lumps of ice on blotting paper and add them, one at a time, to the water.
6. When all the ice has been added, stir until it dissolves and take the final temperature.
7. Find the mass of calorimeter + water + melted ice.

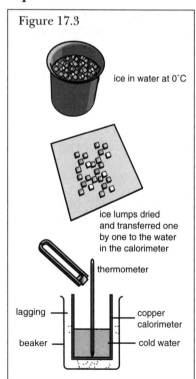

Figure 17.3

ice in water at 0˚C

ice lumps dried and transferred one by one to the water in the calorimeter

thermometer

lagging

beaker

copper calorimeter

cold water

8. The specific latent heat of fusion of ice can be derived from the equation:

Heat needed to melt ice + heat needed to raise the temperature of resulting water = heat lost by calorimeter + heat lost by water.

Warm water makes the ice melt more quickly. The ice is dried so that only ice, not water, is added.

Problem

The following is a set of readings for the above experiment:

Mass of copper calorimeter 50 g, mass of calorimeter + water 145 g, initial temperature 25°C, final temperature 5°C, mass of calorimeter + water + melted ice = 170 g. Find the specific latent heat of fusion of ice.

Table 17.1

heat gained by ice in melting	+ heat to raise resulting water by 5°C	= heat lost by calorimeter	+ heat lost by warm water
$(0.025 \times l)$	$+ (0.025 \times 4,200 \times 5)$	$= (0.05 \times 400 \times 20)$	$+ (0.095 \times 4,200 \times 20)$
$0.025l$	$+ 525$	$= 400$	$+ 7,980$
$0.025l$	$= 8,380 - 525$		
$0.025l$	$= 7,855$		
l	$= 7,855/0.025$	$= 314,200\ J$	$= 314.2\ kJ\ kg^{-1}$

MANDATORY EXPERIMENT

AIM: TO FIND THE SPECIFIC LATENT HEAT OF VAPORISATION OF WATER.

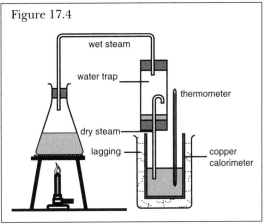

Figure 17.4

Method

1. Weigh the calorimeter. Weigh the calorimeter and water. Take the temperature of the water.
2. Set up the apparatus as shown in Figure 17.4.
3. Allow steam to pass into the water in the calorimeter until the temperature has risen by about 20°C to 25°C.
4. Finally, reweigh the calorimeter and contents to find the mass of steam condensed.
5. The latent heat of vaporisation of water can be derived from the equation: heat lost by steam + heat lost by resulting water = heat gained by calorimeter + heat gained by water

Cooling the water in the calorimeter condenses the steam more efficiently.

Perspiration cools your body. Perspiration consists of salt and water. When the water evaporates it takes its latent heat of vaporisation from your skin and cools you down.

When you put ice in a drink the ice takes its latent heat of fusion from the drink and cools it down.

Impurities raise the boiling point of water.

Reducing the pressure lowers the boiling point of water.

Increasing the pressure raises the boiling point of water.

Increased pressure lowers the melting point of ice.

SUMMARY

- Specific heat capacity: The amount of heat required to raise the temperature of 1 kg of a substance by 1 K.
- The amount of heat gained or lost by a body = mass × specific heat capacity × change of temperature.
- The specific latent heat of fusion of ice is the amount of heat needed to change 1 kg of ice to water without a change of temperature.
- The specific latent heat of vaporisation of water is the amount of heat needed to change 1 kg of water to steam without a change of temperature.
- Reduced pressure lowers the boiling point of water.
- Increased pressure lowers the melting point of ice.

Chapter 18 – Static Electricity

Static electric charges are produced by rubbing together two different materials.

There are two different types of charge – positive and negative.
Like charges repel each other, unlike charges attract each other.

All atoms are made up of three different sorts of sub-atomic particles: protons, neutrons and electrons.

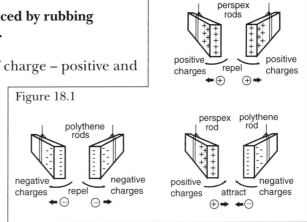

Figure 18.1

Table 18.1

	Proton	Neutron	Electron
Mass	1 a.m.u.	1 a.m.u.	$\frac{1}{1,840}$ a.m.u.
Charge	+1	0	−1
Location	nucleus	nucleus	orbits around nucleus

When you rub two dissimilar substances together one rubs some electrons off the other. When you separate them, one substance has more electrons than it normally should and so is negatively charged; the other has fewer electrons than before and is positively charged.

A body becomes positively charged when it loses electrons.
A body becomes negatively charged when it gains electrons.

CONDUCTORS AND INSULATORS

Conductors are substances through which electric charges can pass freely.

Insulators are substances through which electric charges cannot pass. The charges produced on them cannot move and so stay where they are produced – **static electricity.**

Table 18.2

Conductor	Current carriers	Examples
Solid	Electrons	Copper, aluminium
Liquid	Positive and negative ions	Salt water, copper sulphate solution
Gas	Electrons and ions	Fluorescent and neon gas tubes

ELECTRIC CHARGE

Electric charge (Q) is measured in coulombs.

A coulomb is the quantity of electric charge that passes when a current of one ampere flows for one second.

coulombs = amperes × seconds
$$Q = It$$

The gold leaf electroscope

The gold leaf electroscope is used to:

(a) detect small charges
(b) identify the type of charge – positive or negative
(c) estimate the size of the charge
(d) distinguish between a conductor and insulator.

The only true test of the sign of a charge is when you get an increase in the divergence of the leaf. This tells you that the sign of the test charge is the same as that on the electroscope.

Separating electric charges by induction

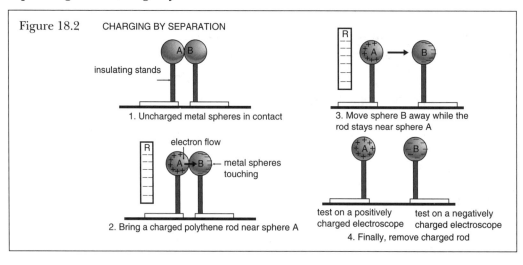

Figure 18.2   CHARGING BY SEPARATION

insulating stands

1. Uncharged metal spheres in contact

electron flow
metal spheres touching

2. Bring a charged polythene rod near sphere A

3. Move sphere B away while the rod stays near sphere A

test on a positively charged electroscope   test on a negatively charged electroscope

4. Finally, remove charged rod

Induction charging by earthing

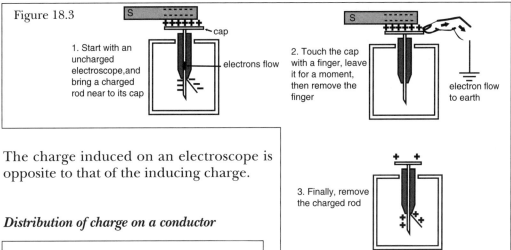

Figure 18.3

1. Start with an uncharged electroscope, and bring a charged rod near to its cap

electrons flow

cap

S

2. Touch the cap with a finger, leave it for a moment, then remove the finger

electron flow to earth

S

The charge induced on an electroscope is opposite to that of the inducing charge.

3. Finally, remove the charged rod

Distribution of charge on a conductor

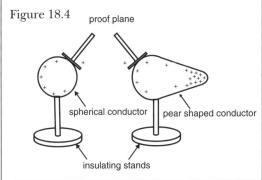

Figure 18.4

proof plane

spherical conductor   pear shaped conductor

insulating stands

Charge on a sphere is uniformly distributed.

Charge on a pear-shaped conductor is concentrated near the pointed end.

The greater the curvature of the conductor (the more pointed it is) the greater the charge density.

Charge is found only on the outside of a charged conductor.

Point discharge

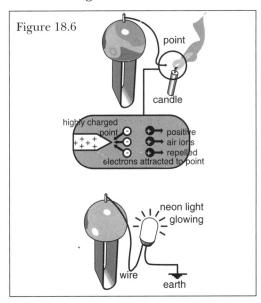

Figure 18.6

point

candle

highly charged point

+ positive air ions repelled

electrons attracted to point

neon light glowing

wire   earth

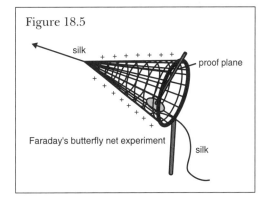

Figure 18.5

silk

proof plane

Faraday's butterfly net experiment

silk

Lightning conductor

A lightning conductor is an earthed conductor with several sharp points at the top fixed to the highest point of a building. It uses point discharge to reduce the effects of electrical storms. The conductor also acts as a low resistance path to the earth if lightning strikes.

Van de Graaff electrostatic generator

The Van de Graaff generator can be charged to a very high voltage.

Large Van de Graaff generators are used to accelerate charged particles in atomic research.

STATIC ELECTRICITY CAUSES PROBLEMS

Static electricity is noticed most when the air is very dry.

The static charge built up when you rub your shoes on a carpet can reach a potential of 20,000 volts. You feel a shock when you are earthed by touching a metal object.

Chemical additives used in fabric conditioners reduce static electricity in clothes.

When refuelling aircraft the friction between the pumps and the fuel causes static charge to build up on the plane. Chemical additives are used to reduce the static and the pumps and plane are connected together and earthed.

SUMMARY

- A body becomes positively charged when it loses electrons.
- A body becomes negatively charged when it gains electrons.
- Conductors are substances through which electric charges can pass freely.
- Insulators are substances through which electric charges cannot pass.

Table 18.3

	Current carriers
Solids	Electrons
Liquids	Positive and negative ions
Gases	Electrons and ions.

- A coulomb is the quantity of electric charge that passes when a current of one ampere flows for one second.
- An electroscope is charged oppositely to the inducing charge.

Chapter 19 – Electric Fields

Coulomb's law: The force between two point charges is directly proportional to the product of the charges and inversely proportional to the square of the distance between them.

$$F \propto \frac{Q_1 \cdot Q_2}{d^2}$$

$$F = \frac{Q_1 \cdot Q_2}{4\pi\varepsilon.d^2}$$

ε is the permittivity of the material between the charges. Permittivity is a property that affects the force between the charges.

Coulomb's law is an example of an **inverse square law.**

Problem 1

Calculate the force a 2 μC charge exerts on a −2 μC charge when 0·01 m apart in a vacuum.

$$F = \frac{Q_1 . Q_2}{4\pi\varepsilon d^2} = \frac{(2 \times 10^{-6}) \cdot (2 \times 10^{-6})}{4\pi \left(\dfrac{10^{-9}}{36\pi}\right)(0 \cdot 01)^2} \qquad \varepsilon_0 = \frac{(10^{-9})}{36\pi}$$

$$= 360 \text{ N}$$

Problem 2

Point charges 20 μC and 60 μC are separated by a 3 mm thick sheet of plastic. If each charge exerts a force of 200×10^3 newtons on the other, calculate the relative permittivity of the plastic.

$$F = \frac{Q_1 \cdot Q_2}{4\pi\varepsilon.d^2}$$

$$\varepsilon = \frac{Q_1.Q_2}{4\pi d^2 F} = \frac{(20 \times 10^{-6})(60 \times 10^{-6})}{4\pi (3 \times 10^{-3})^2.(200 \times 10^3)} = \frac{1 \times 10^{-9}}{6\pi}$$

$$\varepsilon_0 = \frac{(10^{-9})}{36\pi}$$

$$\varepsilon_r = \frac{\varepsilon}{\varepsilon_0} = \frac{1 \times 10^{-9}}{6\pi} \Big/ \frac{(10^{-9})}{36\pi}$$

$$\varepsilon_r = 6$$

Problem 3

Three point charges are arranged as shown in Figure 19.1. What charge must be placed at C so that there is no net force on the charge at B?

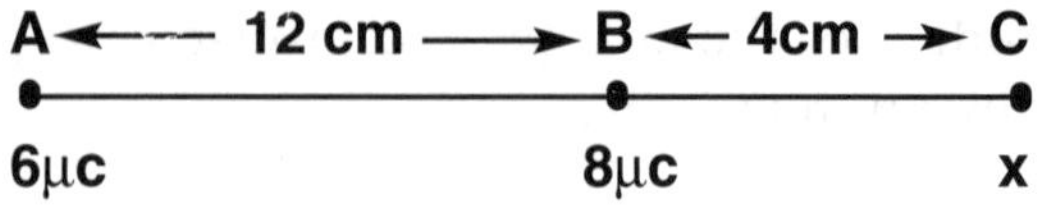

The force exerted on B by A must be balanced by the force exerted on B by C.

Figure 19.1

A ←――― 12 cm ―――→ B ← 4cm → C

6μc   8μc   x

By Coulomb's law, force is directly proportional to the product of the charges and inversely proportional to the square of the distance between them.

$$F_1 \propto \frac{(6\ \mu C)(8\ \mu C)}{12^2}$$

$$F_2 \propto \frac{(8\ \mu C)(x)}{4^2}$$

The forces are balanced so $F_1 = F_2$

$$\frac{(6\ \mu C)(8\ \mu C)}{12^2} = \frac{(8\ \mu C)(x)}{4^2}$$

$$x = \frac{2}{3}\ \mu C$$

ELECTRIC FIELD

An electric field is the space around a charge in which the charge has an effect.

An electric field line is the line along which a positive charge will move when placed in the electric field.

The electric field line gives the vector direction for the electric field.

Field strength

Electric field strength at a point is the force per unit positive charge at that point.

Electric field strength is a vector quantity.

Electric field strength $E = \dfrac{F}{Q}$

The unit of electric field strength is the newton per coulomb (N C^{-1}) or the volt per metre (V m^{-1})

Figure 19.2 demonstrates electric field lines.

Figure 19.2

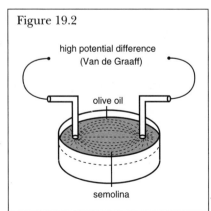

high potential difference
(Van de Graaff)

olive oil

semolina

The electric field strength at P is the force on a unit charge at that point. As there is a charge of 1 unit there:

$$E = \frac{F}{1} = \frac{(Q.1)}{4\pi\varepsilon d^2} \div 1$$

$$= \frac{Q}{4\pi\varepsilon d^2}$$

Electric Flux

The electric flux (ψ) gives a measure of the overall strength of an electric field.

Problem 1

Calculate the electric field strength at a point where a 4 µC charge experiences a force of 0·04 newtons.

The electric field strength at a point is the force on a unit charge at that point.

$$E = \frac{F}{Q}$$

$$= \frac{0\cdot04}{4 \times 10^{-6}}$$

$$= \frac{4 \times 10^{-2}}{4 \times 10^{-6}}$$

$$= 1 \times 10^4 \text{ N C}^{-1}$$

Problem 2

What is the electric field strength at a point 10 cm from a +2 µC point charge?

$$E = \frac{F}{Q}$$

The force between a unit charge and a +2 µC point charge is found by Coulomb's law:

$$F = \left(\frac{1}{4\pi\varepsilon}\right) \cdot \frac{Q.q}{d^2} \text{ where Q is 2 µC and } q \text{ is 1 C (unit charge)}$$

$$= \frac{(1)}{4\pi\left(\dfrac{10^{-9}}{36\pi}\right)} \cdot \frac{(2 \times 10^{-6}).1}{(0\cdot1)^2}$$

$$= 18 \times 10^5 \text{ N}$$
$$= 1\cdot8 \times 10^6 \text{ N}$$

$$E = \frac{F}{q} = \frac{1\cdot8 \times 10^6}{1} = 1\cdot8 \times 10^6 \text{ N C}^{-1}$$

USES OF ELECTRIC FIELDS

The Electrostatic Dust Precipitator removes dust particles from smoke.

A very high voltage electric field moves dust to the plates where it accumulates. The plates are struck regularly by a mechanical hammer and the ash falls into a bin.

Computers have an earthed metal cage around the vulnerable parts to screen them from static discharge. Technicians working on computers earth themselves to discharge any static charges on their bodies before working on the circuit boards.

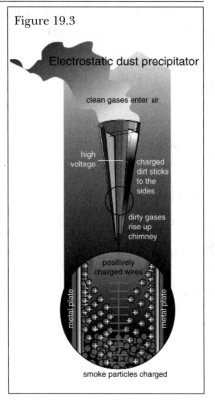

Figure 19.3

Electrostatic dust precipitator

clean gases enter air

high voltage — charged dirt sticks to the sides

dirty gases rise up chimney

positively charged wires

metal plate   metal plate

smoke particles charged

Electric potential

The potential difference between two points is the work done in moving a charge of one coulomb from one point to the other.

Potential difference is measured in volts.

Zero potential

We regard charges a great distance apart as being at zero potential. For practical purposes we take the earth as our zero potential.

A potential difference of one volt exists between two points where one joule of work is done in moving one coulomb between these points.

$$V = \frac{W}{Q}$$

$$\text{volts} = \frac{\text{joules}}{\text{coulombs}}$$

Equipotentials are points at the same potential.

Charge will move only when there is a potential difference between two points and always moves toward the point at lower potential.

Problem 1

2·5 µJ of energy is used to move a 0·5 µC charge between two points. Calculate the potential difference between the points.

$$V = \frac{W}{Q}$$

$$= 2 \cdot 5 \times 10^{-6} / 0 \cdot 5 \times 10^{-6}$$

$$= 5 \text{ volts}$$

Problem 2

Calculate the work done in moving a 3 μC charge from a conductor at a potential
of 20 kV to one at 60 kV.

$$V = \frac{W}{Q}$$

$W = V . Q$ The potential difference is $(60 - 20)$ kV = 40 kV

$\quad = (40 \times 10^3) \cdot (3 \times 10^{-6})$

$\quad = 120 \times 10^{-3}$ J

SUMMARY

- Coulomb's law: The force between two point charges is directly proportional to
  the product of the charges and inversely proportional to the square of the
  distance between them.
- Electric field is the space around a charge in which the charge has an effect.
- Electric field line is the line along which a positive charge will move when placed
  in an electric field.
- Electric field strength at a point is the force per unit positive charge at that
  point.
- Electric flux is a measure of the overall strength of the electric field.
- A potential difference of one volt exists between two points where one joule of
  work is done in moving one coulomb of electric charge between these points.

Chapter 20 – Simple Circuits

Electricity will flow only if there is a complete circuit.

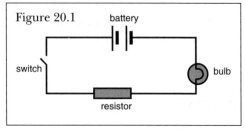

Figure 20.1

ELECTRIC CURRENT

An electric current is a flow of electric charge. Electric current is measured in amperes. When one coulomb of electric charge moves through the circuit in one second the current flow is one ampere.

ampere = coulombs/ seconds

$$I = \frac{Q}{t}$$

ELECTROMOTIVE FORCE (emf)

Batteries (or cells), generators and other sources of electrical energy have emfs.

Electromotive force is the total work done (energy) in moving one coulomb of electric charge round a complete circuit loop.

emf = energy/coulomb = joules/coulomb

$$V = \frac{W}{Q}$$

Problem 1

0·8 mJ of energy is used in moving a 0·5 μC charge from one point to another. Calculate the potential difference between these points.

$$V = \frac{W}{Q}$$
$$= 0\cdot8 \times 10^{-3}/0\cdot5 \times 10^{-6}$$
$$= 1\cdot6 \times 10^3 \text{ V}$$

Problem 2

A total of 90 J of energy is used to move a charge of 15 C around a circuit in 3 seconds. Calculate the potential difference across the circuit and the current flowing.

$$I = \frac{Q}{t} = \frac{15}{3} = 5 \text{ A}$$

$$V = \frac{W}{Q} = \frac{90}{15} = 6 \text{ V}$$

A **potential difference** of one volt exists between any two points when one joule of energy is expended in moving one coulomb between them.

Electricity will flow if there is a potential difference and a complete circuit.

THE SIMPLE CELL

Any combination of two different electrodes in an electrolyte is a simple cell. The simple cell converts chemical energy into electricity.

THE DRY CELL

Dry cells are primary cells and convert chemical energy into electrical energy in a non-reversible way.

Rechargeable cells

Rechargeable cells are secondary cells which means they can be recharged many times.

RESISTANCE

If energy is used in passing electricity through an object that object has a resistance.

MANDATORY EXPERIMENT

AIM: TO INVESTIGATE HOW THE CURRENT FLOWING THROUGH VARIOUS CONDUCTORS VARIES WITH THE POTENTIAL DIFFERENCE APPLIED.

Method

1. Set up the apparatus as shown in Figure 20.2.
2. Set the variable resistor to give a small potential difference (voltage). Note the voltage and current.
3. Adjust the variable resistor to give a slightly larger voltage. Note the voltage and current again.

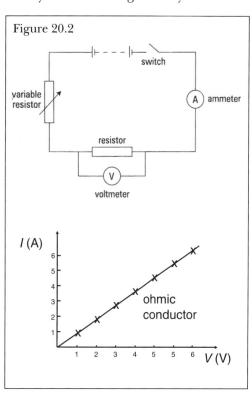

Figure 20.2

4. Repeat this 4 or 5 more times.
5. Draw a graph of voltage (Y axis) against current (X axis).

The ratio of the potential difference applied to the current flowing is constant for a metallic conductor at a constant temperature. This is known as Ohm's law.

Ohm's law: At a constant temperature the current passing through a metallic conductor is directly proportional to the potential difference across it.

Resistance is the ratio of the potential difference across a conductor to the current flowing through it.

$$R = \frac{V}{I}$$

Unit of resistance is the ohm (Ω). The ohm is the resistance of a conductor when a potential difference of 1 volt across it produces a current flow of 1 amp through it.

$$\text{ohms} = \frac{\text{volts}}{\text{amperes}}$$

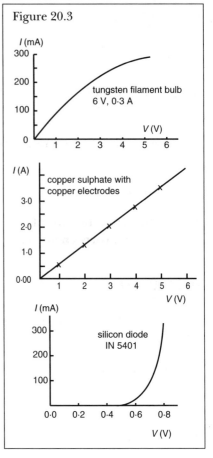

Figure 20.3

All conductors are NOT ohmic (i.e. obey Ohm's law). Semiconductor diodes, thermistors, gases and certain electrolytes are not ohmic.

RHEOSTAT

A rheostat is a variable resistance that controls the current flowing through a circuit. A rheostat is used in circuits where you want to limit the current.

RESISTANCES IN SERIES AND IN PARALLEL

There are some very simple rules for currents and potential differences in circuits.
1. The sum of the currents entering a point in a circuit equals the sum of the currents leaving it. $I = I_1 + I_2 + I_3$
2. The emf of the circuit equals the sum of all the potential differences in the circuit.
   $E = V_1 + V_2 + V_3$

Resistances in series

The two resistors are connected in a line, so the same current I flows through both.

$V = V_1 + V_2$

but $V = IR$ (Ohm's law)

$IR = IR_1 + IR_2$ dividing by I we get

$\mathbf{R = R_1 + R_2}$

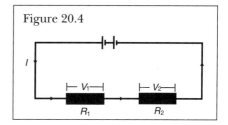

Figure 20.4

Problem

Two resistances of 2 Ω and 4 Ω are connected in series with a 6 V battery. Calculate the potential difference across each resistance.

$R = R_1 + R_2$
$R = 2 + 4 = 6\ \Omega$
$I = \dfrac{V}{R} = \dfrac{6}{6} = 1\ A$

Potential difference across each resistor

$V_1 = IR_1 = 1 \cdot 2 = 2\ V$
$V_2 = IR_2 = 1 \cdot 4 = 4\ V$

Resistances in parallel

The potential difference between two points is the same regardless of the path followed. The potential difference across each of the resistances, from A to B, is V.

$I = I_1 + I_2$

From Ohm's law:

$I = \dfrac{V}{R}$

$\dfrac{V}{R} = \dfrac{V}{R_1} + \dfrac{V}{R_2}$

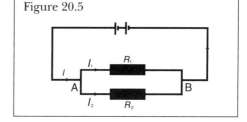

Figure 20.5

dividing by V we get:

$\dfrac{1}{R} = \dfrac{1}{R_1} + \dfrac{1}{R_2}$

Problem 1

A battery of emf 4·5 V and resistance 2·1 Ω is connected to two resistances of 4 Ω and 6 Ω in parallel. Calculate (a) the current flowing through the battery and (b) the potential difference across the two resistors.

The two resistances in parallel:

$$\frac{1}{R} = \frac{1}{R_1} + \frac{1}{R_2}$$

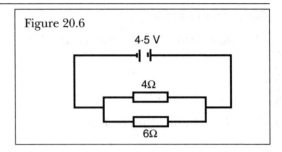

Figure 20.6

$$\frac{1}{R} = \frac{1}{4} + \frac{1}{6} = \frac{5}{12}$$

$$R = \frac{12}{5} = 2\cdot4\ \Omega$$

This resistance is in series with the battery resistance:

$$R = R_1 + R_2$$

$$R = 2\cdot4 + 2\cdot1 = 4\cdot5\ \Omega$$

$$I = \frac{V}{R} = \frac{4\cdot5}{4\cdot5} = 1\ \text{A} \quad \text{answer (a)}$$

The potential difference across the two resistors:

$$V = IR = 1 \times 2\cdot4 = 2\cdot4\ \text{V} \quad \text{answer (b)}$$

Problem 2

A battery of emf 10 V is connected across three resistances arranged as shown in Figure 20.7.
   Calculate:

(a) the total resistance in the circuit,
(b) the current flowing through the 3 Ω resistance,
(c) the voltage across the 3 Ω resistance,
(d) the voltage across the 8 Ω resistance.

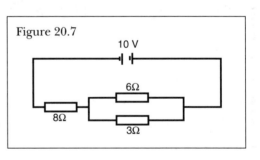

Figure 20.7

The 6 Ω and 3 Ω resistances are in parallel.

$$\frac{1}{R} = \frac{1}{R_1} + \frac{1}{R_2}$$

$$\frac{1}{R} = \frac{1}{6} + \frac{1}{3} = \frac{3}{6}$$

$$R = \frac{6}{3} = 2\ \Omega$$

This equivalent resistance and the 8 Ω resistance are in series.

Total resistance in circuit: $R = R_1 + R_2$

$$R = 2 + 8 = 10\ \Omega \ \text{(a)}$$

Total current flowing in circuit: $I = \dfrac{V}{R} = \dfrac{10}{10} = 1$ A

Potential difference across 8 Ω resistance: $V = I.R = 1.8 = 8$ V (d)

The rest of the voltage is across the two resistances in parallel = 2 V

Voltage across the 3 Ω resistance = 2 V (c)

Current through 3 Ω resistance: $I = \dfrac{V}{R} = \dfrac{2}{3} = \dfrac{2}{3}$ A (b)

ELECTRICITY IN THE HOME

Ring main circuit

In a ring main circuit the live and neutral wires each form a ring or loop. A third loop is formed by the earth wire. This gives two independent paths for the current to any point and reduces the thickness of wire needed.

Switch

The live wire is always connected through the switch.

Fuse

If a circuit becomes overloaded (too big a current), the fuse wire melts and breaks the circuit.

Miniature circuit breaker (MCB) or trip switch

This circuit breaker is a mechanical alternative to a fuse that cuts off the current when the current exceeds a particular value.

Earthing gives a low resistance path to earth.

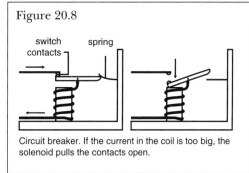

Figure 20.8

switch contacts spring

Circuit breaker. If the current in the coil is too big, the solenoid pulls the contacts open.

Bonding

Bonding ensures that there is always an unbroken low resistance path for the current to flow to earth by connecting all the metal objects in a bathroom – pipes, metal parts of shower and bath – to a good earth.

Double insulated appliances

Double insulated appliances have all live connections insulated and all metal parts are also insulated.

Residual current device (RCD) or earth leakage circuit breaker (ELCB)

The RCD is a trip switch that cuts off the current very quickly when a fault in an appliance causes a small current to flow to earth.

SAFETY

Fuses, switches, earthing, bonding and RCDs help improve the electrical safety of your home.

SUMMARY

- An electric current is a flow of electric charge.
- Electromotive force (emf) is the total work done in moving one coulomb of electric charge round a complete circuit loop.
- A potential difference of one volt exists between two points when one joule of energy is expended in moving one coulomb of electric charge between them.
- Electricity will flow if there is a potential difference and a complete circuit.
- Any combination of two different electrodes in an electrolyte is a simple cell.
- Ohm's law: At a constant temperature the current passing through a metallic conductor is directly proportional to the potential difference across it.
- Resistance is the ratio of the potential difference across a conductor to the current flowing through it.
- The ohm is the resistance of a conductor such that a potential difference of one volt across it produces a current flow of one ampere through it.
- Resistances in series: $R = R_1 + R_2$
- Resistances in parallel: $\dfrac{1}{R} = \dfrac{1}{R_1} + \dfrac{1}{R_2}$
- If energy is used in passing electricity through an object that object has a resistance.

Chapter 21 – Magnetism and Magnetic Fields

A magnet is a piece of iron, cobalt or nickel (or alloys of these) that can attract other pieces of the same metals.

When a magnet is free to swing it settles in a north-south direction.

A compass contains a magnetic needle that always comes to rest pointing in a north-south direction.

FORCES BETWEEN MAGNETS

Like magnetic poles repel. Unlike magnetic poles attract.

MAGNETIC FIELDS

A magnetic field is the space within which a magnetic force has an effect.

Plotting the magnetic field round a bar magnet, *see* Figure 21.2.

Magnetic field line

The path along which a north pole would move if it were free to do so.

MAGNETIC EFFECT OF AN ELECTRIC CURRENT

A conductor carrying an electric current has a magnetic effect.

Mapping the magnetic field patterns of (a) a straight conductor, (b) a loop and (c) a solenoid.

(a) a straight conductor

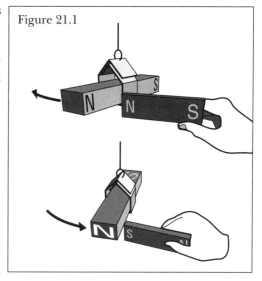

Figure 21.1

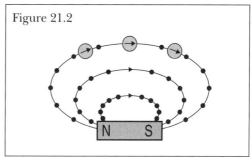

Figure 21.2

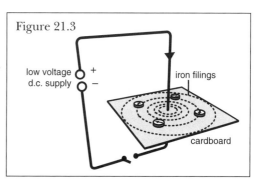

Figure 21.3

low voltage d.c. supply

+
−

iron filings

cardboard

Right-hand grip rule for the direction of the magnetic field around a straight current-carrying conductor.

Hold your right hand with your thumb pointing along the direction in which the current flows. The direction that your fingers (your grip) point gives the direction of the magnetic field lines.

(b) a loop

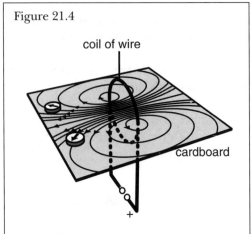

Figure 21.4

coil of wire

cardboard

(c) a solenoid

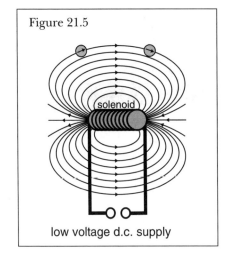

Figure 21.5

solenoid

low voltage d.c. supply

MAGNETIC FLUX

The total magnetic flux depends on the strength of the magnet that produces the flux. Magnetic flux (Φ) is measured in webers (Wb).

Magnetic flux density (B) is the magnetic flux per unit area at right angles to the direction of the magnetic field lines.

The unit of magnetic flux density is the tesla (T) or weber per square metre, (Wb m^{-2}). Magnetic flux density is a vector. The direction of the magnetic flux density is the direction of the field lines through the area.

MAKING MAGNETS

Place a steel bar inside a solenoid (long coil of wire) and pass a large direct current through the wire.

DEMAGNETISING

Heating or hammering a magnet will destroy its magnetism. You can demagnetise an object that has become magnetic by induction through being in contact with strong magnets by passing alternating current (a.c.) through a solenoid containing the object and then slowly withdrawing the object.

MAGNETIC TAPES

Audio and video tapes are used to store information (e.g. music, films, etc.). The plastic tape is coated with iron oxide particles. The recorder converts the information into electric pulses. The pulses magnetise the iron oxide particles into a pattern that represents the information. When the tape is replayed the pattern is converted back to electric pulses that are then converted back to sound (and pictures).

USES OF MAGNETS

Magnets are used as catches on cupboard doors. Magnetic seals are used on fridge doors. Magnets are also used in electric motors, loudspeakers and dynamos. Electromagnets are used on cranes in scrapyards, in relays and in electric doorbells.

SUMMARY

- A freely suspended magnet will settle in a north-south direction.
- Like magnetic poles repel, unlike magnetic poles attract.
- Iron, nickel, cobalt and steel can be magnetised.
- The space within which a magnet has an effect is called its magnetic field.
- A magnetic line of force is the path along which a north pole would move.
- Right-hand grip rule for the direction of the magnetic field around a current-carrying conductor. Hold your right hand with your thumb pointing along the direction in which the current flows. The direction your fingers point (your grip) gives the direction of the magnetic field lines.
- Right-hand grip rule for the direction of the magnetic field in the centre of a current-carrying loop or a solenoid. Point the fingers (grip) of your right hand along the direction in which the current flows through the coil or solenoid. Your thumb now points in the direction of the magnetic field.

Chapter 22 – Measuring Resistances

An ohmmeter uses Ohm's law to measure resistance. A cell of known emf is connected to an ammeter. The leads X and Y are connected across the unknown resistance R. The current passing through R is measured by the ammeter.

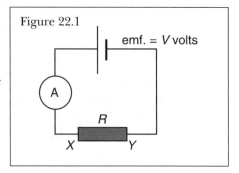

Figure 22.1

From Ohm's law: $R = \dfrac{V}{I}$

The emf of the cell is taken as V: by measuring I we get a value for R.

RESISTANCE OF A METALLIC CONDUCTOR

R is proportional to l.
R is inversely proportional to A
(Where A is the cross-sectional area of the wire.)

$$R \propto \frac{l}{A}$$
$$R = \frac{k.l}{A}$$

The constant k depends on the material of the wire called the resistivity (ρ) of the metal.

$$R = \frac{\rho.l}{A}$$
$$\rho = \frac{RA}{l}$$

Unit of resistivity: ohm metre = Ω m

Problem 1

A piece of wire has a length of 68·5 cm. The diameter of the wire is 0·20 mm and its resistance is 26·4 Ω. Calculate the resistivity of the material of the wire.

$$\rho = \frac{RA}{l}$$
$$= \frac{(26\cdot4)\pi(0\cdot10 \times 10^{-3})^2}{68\cdot5 \times 10^{-2}}$$
$$= 1\cdot21 \times 10^{-6} \ \Omega \ m$$

Problem 2

The resistance of a length of wire is 19 Ω. Its diameter is 2 mm and the resistivity of the material of the wire is 1×10^{-6} Ω m. Calculate the length of the wire.

$$l \;=\; \frac{RA}{\rho} \;=\; \frac{(19)\pi(1{\cdot}0 \times 10^{-3})^2}{1 \times 10^{-6}} \;=\; 59{\cdot}69 \text{ m}$$

MANDATORY EXPERIMENT

AIM: TO MEASURE THE RESISTIVITY OF THE MATERIAL OF A WIRE.

Method

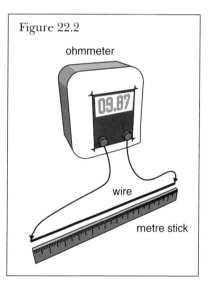

Figure 22.2

1. Connect the wire to a digital ohmmeter and measure the exact length of nichrome wire between the terminals.
2. Measure the resistance of the wire with an ohmmeter.
3. Measure the diameter of the wire at a number of places with the micrometer screw gauge. Take the average of these as the diameter. (Check the micrometer for zero error.) Calculate the cross-sectional area of the wire. Assume that it is perfectly circular $(A = \pi r^2)$.
4. Calculate the resistivity of the material from the formula: $\rho = \dfrac{RA}{l}$.

RESISTANCE VARIES WITH TEMPERATURE

The resistance of a material varies with temperature. For most metals the resistance increases with temperature. For semiconductors such as silicon and germanium the resistance decreases with temperature. The resistance of alloys such as magnanin does not vary appreciably with temperature.

MANDATORY EXPERIMENT

AIM: TO INVESTIGATE HOW THE RESISTANCE OF A METALLIC CONDUCTOR VARIES WITH TEMPERATURE.

Method

1. Set up the apparatus as shown in Figure 22.3.
2. Heat the water slowly to raise the temperature to about 90°C.
3. Measure the resistance of the wire with the digital ohmmeter.
4. Note the temperature.

5. Measure the resistance at temperature intervals of 10°C as the temperature of the wire resistor falls. Note the temperature of the water each time.
6. Plot a graph of R against θ.

The resistance of a metallic conductor varies directly with temperature.

Thermistors

A thermistor is a semiconductor device whose resistance changes greatly with a change in temperature. They are usually metal oxides of copper, nickel or cobalt. The resistance changes from about 400 Ω at room temperature to about 40 Ω when hot.

A thermistor is a semiconductor device whose resistance changes greatly with temperature.

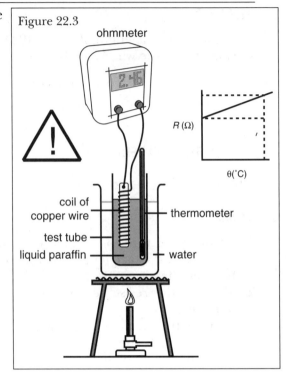

Figure 22.3

MANDATORY EXPERIMENT

AIM: TO INVESTIGATE HOW THE RESISTANCE OF A THERMISTOR VARIES WITH TEMPERATURE.

Method

1. Set up the apparatus as shown in Figure 22.4.
2. Heat the water slowly to raise the temperature to about 90°C.
3. Measure the resistance of the thermistor with the digital ohmmeter.
4. Note the temperature.
5. Measure the resistance at temperature intervals of 10°C as the temperature of the thermistor falls. Note the temperature of the water each time.
6. Plot a graph of R against θ.

Thermistors are used as heat sensors.

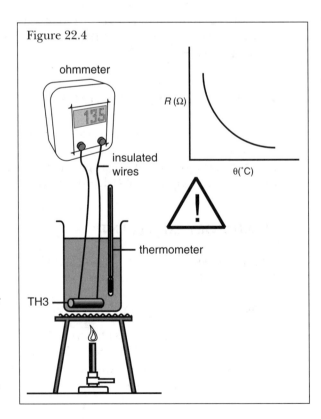

Figure 22.4

LIGHT-DEPENDENT RESISTOR (LDR)

A light-dependent resistor (LDR) is a semiconductor whose resistance changes with the amount of light falling on it.

The resistance of the cadmium sulphide (CdS) light-dependent resistor is about 10 MΩ in the dark and falls to about 1 kΩ in normal daylight.

WHEATSTONE BRIDGE

The Wheatstone bridge circuit measures resistance by comparing an unknown resistance with a known standard resistance. As no current flows through the galvanometer from one arm of the bridge to the other the accuracy of the galvanometer does not matter.

When the Wheatstone bridge is balanced, no current flows through the galvanometer. This means that there is no potential difference between B and C. B is at the same potential as C.

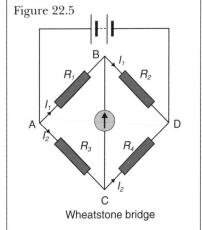

Figure 22.5

Wheatstone bridge

The current flowing in AB = current in BD.
$$I_1 R_1 = I_2 R_3$$

The current flowing in AC = current in CD.
$$I_1 R_2 = I_2 R_4$$

Dividing we get
$$\frac{I_1 R_1}{I_1 R_2} = \frac{I_2 R_3}{I_2 R_4}$$

$$\frac{R_1}{R_2} = \frac{R_3}{R_4}$$

The ratio of resistances R_1 and R_2 is usually a power of ten (10, 100 etc.). R_3 is a variable resistance that can be set at known values. R_4 is the resistance being measured.

Problem 1

A Wheatstone bridge circuit is balanced when $R_1 = 1\ \Omega$, $R_2 = 1{,}000\ \Omega$ and $R_3 = 694\ \Omega$. What is the resistance of the fourth resistor?

$$\frac{R_1}{R_2} = \frac{R_3}{R_4}$$

$$\frac{1}{1{,}000} = \frac{694}{X}$$

$$X \quad = \quad 694{,}000 \quad = \quad 694\ \text{k}\Omega$$

Problem 2

A Wheatstone bridge circuit is balanced when $R_1 = 1{,}000\ \Omega$, $R_2 = 1\ \Omega$, $R_3 = 248\ \Omega$ and $R_4 = 0{\cdot}5\ \Omega$. Is the bridge balanced?

$$\frac{R_1}{R_2} = \frac{R_3}{R_4}$$

$$\frac{1{,}000}{1} = \frac{248}{X}$$

$1{,}000\ X = 248$
$X = 0{\cdot}248\ \Omega$
$X \neq R_4$

The bridge is not balanced.

USES OF THE WHEATSTONE BRIDGE

Strain gauges

Any strain increases the length of the wire and so increases its resistance.

Fire alarm

A fire affects the thermistor nearest the fire far more than the other. This unbalances the Wheatstone bridge and sets off an alarm.

Thermostat

The Wheatstone bridge circuit can also be used to maintain a steady temperature in an oven.

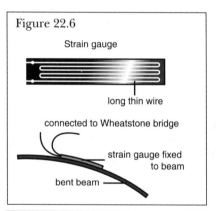

Figure 22.6

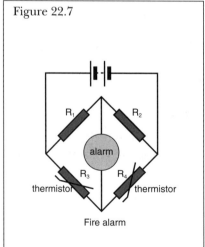

Figure 22.7

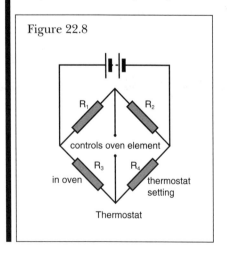

Figure 22.8

Fail safe device

If the pilot flame goes out the thermistor goes cold, its resistance increases and the bridge is now unbalanced. The p.d. across the bridge operates a solenoid and shuts off the fuel.

POTENTIAL DIVIDER

We can get a variety of different voltages from a single voltage supply by using a potential divider.

Problem

Calculate the potential difference (voltage) across each of the resistors shown in Figure 22.10.

The resistors are in series.

Total resistance = 3 + 6 = 9 Ω

Current flowing through the circuit:

$$I = \frac{V}{R} = \frac{12}{9} = \frac{4}{3} \text{ A}$$

p.d. across 3 resistor: $V = IR = \frac{4}{3} \times 3 = 4 \text{ V}$

p.d. across 6 resistor: $V = IR = \frac{4}{3} \times 6 = 8 \text{ V}$

Clearly the supply voltage was divided between the two resistors in proportion to their resistances.

Although the rheostat and potential divider look alike – and frequently the same device can be connected to one circuit as a rheostat and to another circuit as a potential divider – it is important to realise that the principle of operation is not the same.

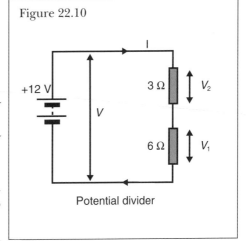

Figure 22.9

fuel input valve

thermistor   thermistor

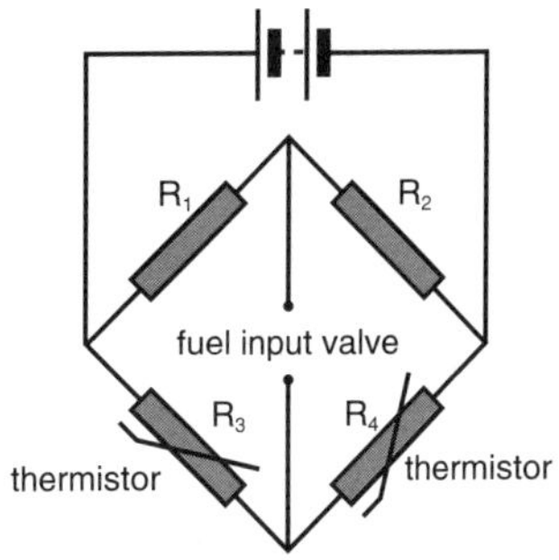

Flame sensor
(fail safe device)

Figure 22.10

+12 V

Potential divider

SUMMARY

- The resistance of a metallic conductor varies directly with temperature.
- **A thermistor is a semiconductor device whose resistance changes greatly with temperature.**
- The resistance of a thermistor falls sharply with increasing temperature.
- A light-dependent resistor is a semiconductor whose resistance changes with the amount of light falling on it.

Chapter 23 – The Heating and Chemical Effects of an Electric Current

HEATING EFFECT

Joule's law: The heat produced in a fixed time for a given resistance is proportional to the current squared.

$$H \propto I^2$$

The heating effect is also proportional to the resistance and the time:

$$H = I^2 R t$$

POWER

The power is the energy produced or consumed per second. The unit of power is the watt (W).

$$\text{power} = \frac{\text{energy}}{\text{seconds}}$$

$$P = \frac{J}{t} = \frac{I^2 R t}{t} = I^2 R = V.I$$

watts = volts × amps

$$P = V.I$$

Problem 1

A heating element is rated at 25 W and has a resistance of 100 Ω. What is the maximum current you can safely pass through this heater? What is the voltage across the resistance?

$$P = V.I = I^2 R$$

$$I^2 = \frac{P}{R} = \frac{25}{100} = \frac{1}{4}$$

$$I = \frac{1}{2} \text{ A}$$

$$V = I.R = \frac{1}{2} \cdot 100 = 50 \text{ V}$$

Problem 2

The supply cables to a cooker can safely carry 60 A. The cooker is rated as 12 kW at 220 V. Can the cables carry the current safely when fully switched on?

$P = V.I$

$12,000 = 220.I$

$I = \dfrac{12,000}{220} = 54 \cdot 5 \text{ A}$

The cables can carry this current safely.

Problem 3

An electric kettle holds 1 kg of water when full. It is rated as 1,200 W at 220 V. How long does the full kettle take to come to the boil if the tap water is at 20°C. (Boiling point of water is 100°C and its specific heat capacity is 4,200 J kg^{-1} K^{-1}.)

electrical energy $= VIt = P.t$
heat $= m.c.\Delta\theta = $ electrical energy
$P.t = m.c.\Delta\theta$
$1,200.t = 1.4,200.80$
$t = 280 \text{ s}$

MANDATORY EXPERIMENT

AIM: TO VERIFY JOULE'S LAW.

Method

1. Set up the apparatus as shown in Figure 23.1.
2. Add enough water to cover the heating element in the calorimeter. Note the temperature of the water.
3. Pass a current of 0·5 A through the heating coil. Keep the current constant by adjusting the rheostat.
4. Note the temperature rise after 5 minutes.
5. Repeat by passing the currents of 1 A, 1·5 A, 2 A, 2·5 A, 3 A successively through the heating coil for 5 minutes. Note the temperature rise for each current.

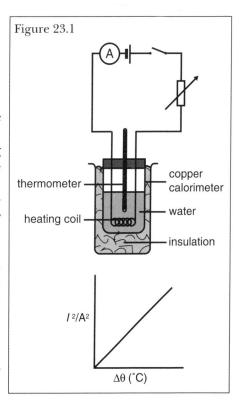

Figure 23.1

thermometer

copper calorimeter

heating coil

water

insulation

I^2/A^2

$\Delta\theta$ (°C)

The heat energy produced is the mass multiplied by specific heat capacity by rise in temperature.

$$H = m.c.\Delta\theta$$

As the mass and specific heat capacity are constant

$$H \propto \Delta\theta$$

6. Draw a graph of the temperature rise $\Delta\theta$ against I^2 (the square of the current). The result is a straight line through the origin.

Conclusion: The heat produced in a given time for a fixed resistance is proportional to the current squared.

The ESB transfers energy at a high voltage

Heat loss due to current flowing through the cables, by Joule's law, depends on the current squared and the resistance. The resistance is constant, so the heat loss depends on the square of the current. To minimise heat loss it makes sense to keep the current low. This can only be done by transmission at high voltage.

THE KILOWATT HOUR

A one kilowatt appliance left on for one hour uses one kilowatt hour of electrical energy.

kilowatt hours = kilowatts × hours

Problem 1

How much does it cost to run a 2 kW electric fire for three hours if one unit (kilowatt hour) costs 10·2c?

kilowatt hours = kilowatts × hours
2 kilowatts × 3 hours = 6 kilowatt hours
6 units @ 10·2c = 61·2c

Problem 2

You are going away on holiday and think of leaving on a 25 W light. If you are away for 7 days how much will it cost if one unit costs 10·2c.

$$25 \text{ W} = \frac{25}{1,000} = 0 \cdot 025 \text{ kW}$$
0·025 kilowatts × (7 × 24) hours = 4·2 kilowatt hours
4·2 units @ 10·2c = 42·8c

CHEMICAL EFFECT: ELECTROLYSIS

Electric current is carried through the solution by the movement of ions.

An electrolyte is a substance that, molten or in solution, conducts electricity by the movement of ions.

Electrolysis is the process of causing chemical changes by passing an electric current through an electrolyte.

Commercial uses of electrolysis

Electrolytic refining of metals and electroplating.

Electrolytes obey Ohm's law when precautions are taken to exclude any 'back' emfs.

CuSO$_4$ with copper electrodes: This obeys Ohm's law as the copper ions discharged at the cathode are immediately replaced by copper atoms entering the solution as ions at the anode.

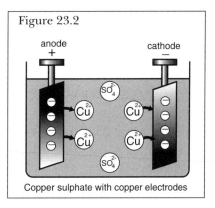

Figure 23.2

Copper sulphate with copper electrodes

CuSO$_4$ with inert (platinum) electrodes: This does not follow Ohm's law as oxygen is produced at the anode. The oxygen and the platinum electrode produce a 'back' emf that must be overcome before current will flow.

SUMMARY

• Joule's law: The heat produced in a fixed time for a given resistance is proportional to the current squared.
• Power: The energy produced or consumed per second.
• watts = volts × amperes
• Electricity is transmitted at high voltage to reduce energy losses due to heat.
• Kilowatt hours equal kilowatts multiplied by hours.
• An electrolyte is a substance which, molten or in solution, conducts electricity by the movement of ions.
• Electrolysis is the process of causing a chemical reaction by passing an electric current through an electrolyte.

Chapter 24 – The Force on a Current-carrying Conductor in a Magnetic Field

Figure 24.1 demonstrates that there is a force on a current-carrying conductor in a magnetic field.

A current-carrying conductor in a magnetic field experiences a force.

This is shown in Figure 24.2. The force depends on the current, the length of the conductor in the magnetic field and the magnetic flux density through the conductor at right angles.

$F = IlB$

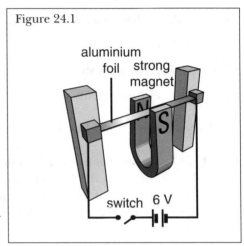

Figure 24.1

aluminium foil   strong magnet

switch   6 V

Problem 1

A straight horizontal wire of length 0·20 m carrying a current of 10 A is perpendicular to a magnetic field of flux density 0·60 tesla. What is the force acting on the wire?

$F = IlB$
$\quad = (10)(0·20)(0·60)$
$\quad = 1·2$ N

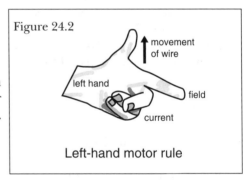

Figure 24.2

movement of wire

left hand   field

current

Left-hand motor rule

Problem 2

A current flowing through a conductor at right angles to a magnetic field experiences a force of 1·5 N. If the wire is 20 cm long and carries a current of 5 A, what is the strength of the magnetic field?

$F = IlB$
$B = \dfrac{F}{Il} = \dfrac{1·5}{(0·20)(5)} = 1·5$ tesla

Applications:
Moving-coil loudspeakers, electric motors and moving-coil meters all work on the principle that there is a force on a current-carrying conductor in a magnetic field.

Conductor not perpendicular to magnetic field

It is only the component of the magnetic field perpendicular to the current that produces a force on the conductor. This component is B sin θ where θ is the angle between the conductor and the magnetic field lines.

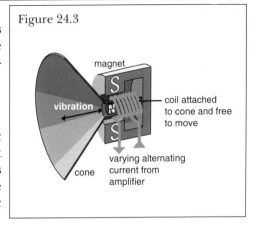

Figure 24.3

magnet

vibration

cone

coil attached to cone and free to move

varying alternating current from amplifier

MAGNETIC FLUX DENSITY

The force on a current-carrying conductor in a magnetic field can be used to measure the strength of the magnetic field: the magnetic flux density.

Magnetic flux density $B = \dfrac{F}{Il}$ (The force acting per unit current length.)

The magnetic flux density (B) is one tesla when a current of one ampere flowing through a conductor of length one metre in a magnetic field produces a force of one newton.

Force on a moving charge in a magnetic field

The force on a conductor in a magnetic field is

$$F = IlB$$

The current flowing through the conductor is made up of n individual charges of q coulombs moving with an average velocity of v m s^{-1}. The total charge $Q = nq$.

$F = IlB$ but $I = \dfrac{Q}{t}$ where Q is the total charge

$F = \dfrac{QlB}{t}$ but $Q = nq$

$F = \dfrac{nqlB}{t}$ but $\dfrac{l}{t} = v$ the average velocity of the charges

$F = nqvB$

This is the force on n charges. The force on a single charge $F = qvB$.

Problem

An electron, charge 1.6×10^{-19} C is travelling at a velocity of 5×10^5 m s^{-1} at right angles to a magnetic field of flux density 3 T. What is the force on the electron?

$$F = qvB$$
$$= (1.6 \times 10^{-19})(5 \times 10^5)(3)$$
$$= 24 \times 10^{-14}$$
$$= 2.4 \times 10^{-13} \text{ N}$$

Forces between currents

Figure 24.4 shows that there are forces between electric currents.

When current flows in the same direction the conductors are attracted toward each other.

When current flows in opposite directions the conductors repel each other.

The unit of electric current, the ampere, is defined in terms of the force between currents.

The ampere is that constant current which, if maintained in two infinitely long conductors of negligible cross-section one metre apart in a vacuum, would produce between the conductors a force of 2×10^{-7} newtons per metre length.

Figure 24.4

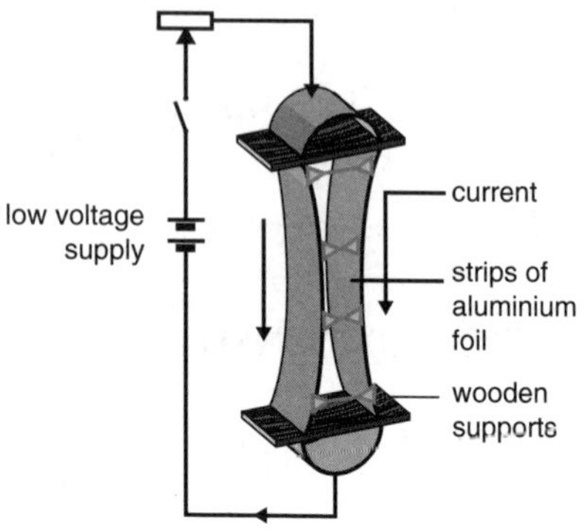

Currents in the *same* direction *attract* each other

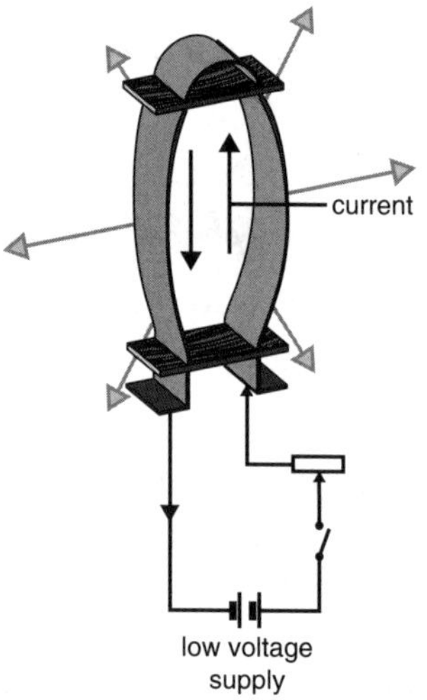

Currents in *opposite* directions *repel* each other

SUMMARY

* A current-carrying conductor in a magnetic field experiences a force.
* The magnetic flux density (B) is one tesla when a current of one ampere flowing through a conductor of length one metre in a magnetic field produces a force of one newton.
* Magnetic flux density (B) is the magnetic flux per unit area at right angles to the direction of the magnetic field lines.
* The ampere is that constant current which, if maintained in two infinitely long conductors of negligible cross-section one metre apart in a vacuum, would produce between the conductors a force of 2×10^{-7} newtons per metre length.
* $F = IlB$
* $F = qvB$

Chapter 25 – Applied Electricity: Current and Magnetic Fields (Option 2)

ELECTROMAGNETIC RELAY

An electromagnetic relay is a device that enables a small current in one circuit to switch on (or off) a large current in an adjoining circuit.

Lights and heated windows in a car are all switched on using electromagnetic relays.

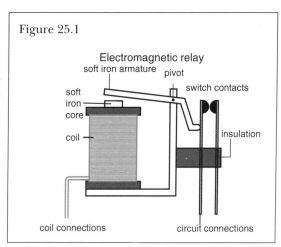

Figure 25.1

Electromagnetic relay

SIMPLE D.C. MOTOR

The d.c. motor consists of a rectangular coil of wire wound on a frame of laminated soft iron. This is mounted on a shaft so that it can rotate between the concave pole faces of a magnet. The ends of the coil are connected to a copper split-ring commutator. This is attached to the coil and rotates with it. Two fixed carbon brushes press lightly against the commutator. When these are connected to a battery, current flows through the coil and the coil rotates.

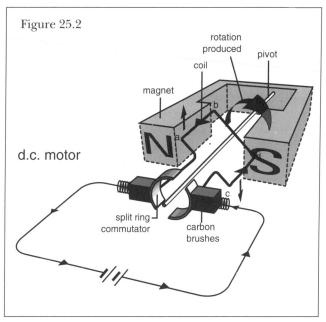

Figure 25.2

d.c. motor

Radial magnetic field

A soft iron cylinder placed between the concave pole pieces produces a uniform radial field. A coil pivoted about the centre will lie along the direction of the field lines in all positions.

Motors and 'back' emf

The coil of the motor generates an emf when it turns. This emf acts in a direction opposite to that of the battery that supplies current to the motor. It is known as a 'back' emf as its effect is to slow down the motor.

The 'back' emf (E) depends on the speed of revolution of the motor.

An electric motor regulates its speed with the load on it

When a load is applied to a motor the speed decreases. This reduces the 'back' emf so the current flowing through the motor increases and gives a greater torque.

Simple d.c. motors are used in tape recorders, video recorders, automatic cameras and starter motors in cars.

LOUDSPEAKERS

The principle of a moving coil loudspeaker is that a current-carrying conductor in a magnetic field experiences a force that moves a cone at the frequency of the current.

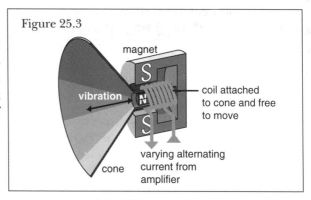

Figure 25.3

MOVING COIL METERS

A galvanometer is made of a coil of fine wire wound on an aluminium frame. The coil is pivoted on bearings and carries a pointer. A fixed soft iron cylinder and a magnet with concave pole faces produce a radial magnetic field. The current to and from the coil goes through hairsprings.

When current flows through the coil it produces a couple that turns it. The hairsprings produce

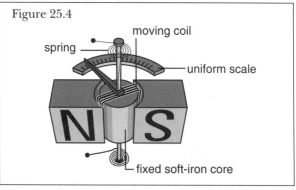

Figure 25.4

an opposing couple when turned. This opposing couple depends on the spring used and the angle (θ) through which it is turned.

The couple produced by the coil $T_1 = nIAB$
The opposing couple due to the spring $T_2 = k\theta$
When the pointer is at rest:

$T_1 = T_2$
$nIAB = k\theta$

As n, B, A and k are constants

$I \propto \theta$

The principle of the moving coil galvanometer is that a current-carrying conductor in a magnetic field experiences a force.

Sensitivity of the galvanometer

A sensitive meter produces a large angular deflection (θ) for a small current (I). $\underline{\theta}$ should be big.
I

$$\frac{\theta}{I} = \frac{nAB}{k}$$

A sensitive galvanometer is made by using: (a) a strong magnet, B is large; (b) a coil of many turns, n is big; (c) a coil of large area, A is large; (d) a weak spring, k is small.

Damping

The coil of the galvanometer is wound on an aluminium frame to 'damp' the movement of the coil and bring the pointer quickly to rest. The frame produces a 'back' emf when it cuts through the magnetic field and slows down the coil.

Ammeter

A galvanometer is converted to an ammeter by connecting a small resistance in parallel with it.

Problem

A galvanometer has a resistance of 5 Ω and gives a full-scale deflection with a current of 10 mA. What resistance must be connected in parallel to enable the galvanometer to measure currents up to 1 A?

10 mA is the maximum current that can pass through the galvanometer.
990 mA must pass through the parallel resistor – the 'shunt' resistance.
The voltage across each resistance is the same:

$(10 \times 10^{-3})(5) = (990 \times 10^{-3})(R)$
$R = 0.05$ Ω

In theory, the resistance of the ammeter should be zero. In practice the resistance of the ammeter is as small as possible.

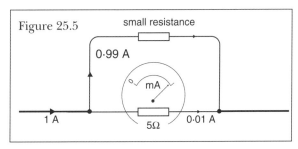
Figure 25.5

Voltmeter

A galvanometer is converted to a voltmeter by connecting a large resistance in series.

Problem

A galvanometer has a resistance of 5 Ω and gives a full-scale deflection with a current of 10 mA. What resistance must be connected in series to enable the galvanometer measure a voltage of 5 V?

10 mA is the maximum current that can pass through the galvanometer.
5 V is the maximum voltage you want to measure.
   The total resistance: $R = \dfrac{V}{I} = 5/10 \times 10^{-3} = 500 \ \Omega$

   The galvanometer has a resistance of 5 Ω so the series resistor must supply the other 495 Ω

   Series resistance = 495 Ω

In theory, the resistance of the voltmeter should be infinitely large and so allow no current through the voltmeter. In practice it as large as possible.

Limitations of moving coil meters

The moving coil galvanometer cannot measure alternating current (a.c.).
   Only small currents can be measured directly because of the fine wire in the coil.
   The moving iron type of meter is more robust and can measure both a.c. and d.c. currents.

Ohmmeter

A galvanometer is converted to an ohmmeter by connecting a dry cell (1·5 V) in series with a series resistor R_s. The series resistor is necessary to ensure that too big a current does not flow through the galvanometer. There is also an adjusting resistor R_a that allows you to compensate for changes in the emf of the battery as it ages.

Figure 25.6   Ohmmeter

   The ohmmeter scale is not linear and it is not an accurate instrument, often having an error of 10%.
   Ohmmeters are used:

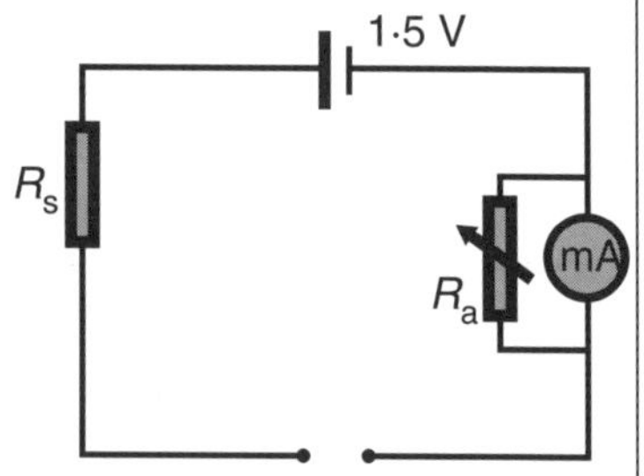

(i) to test a circuit for continuity – to ensure that there are no breaks in a circuit
(ii) to get approximate values of resistances.

SUMMARY

- An electromagnetic relay is a device that enables a small current in one circuit to switch on (or off) a large current in an adjoining circuit.
- The principle of the moving coil loudspeaker is that a current-carrying conductor in a magnetic field experiences a force.
- The principle of moving coil galvanometer is that a current-carrying conductor in a magnetic field experiences a force.
- A galvanometer is converted to an ammeter by connecting a small resistance parallel to it.
- A galvanometer is converted to a voltmeter by connecting a large resistance in series with it.

Chapter 26 – Electromagnetic Induction

Relative movement between a magnet and a coil causes an electric current to flow in the coil.

Electromagnetic induction means that an emf is induced whenever the magnetic flux cutting a conductor changes.

Faraday's law: Whenever there is a change in the magnetic flux cutting a circuit, an emf is induced, the strength of which is proportional to the rate of change of flux cutting the circuit.

Lenz's law: The direction of the induced emf is always such as to oppose the change causing it.

Electromagnetic induction is a conversion of mechanical energy into electrical energy

The unit of magnetic flux – the weber – is defined by electromagnetic induction.

The weber (Wb): is the magnetic flux which, linking a circuit of one turn, produces in it an emf of one volt as the flux is reduced to zero at a uniform rate in one second.

The flux through an area of 1 m² is one weber if the flux density in this area is one tesla.

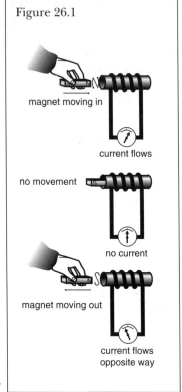

Figure 26.1

magnet moving in

current flows

no movement

no current

magnet moving out

current flows opposite way

Faraday's law may be stated mathematically as:

$$E = -\frac{d\phi}{dt}$$

where E is the emf induced, $\frac{d\phi}{dt}$ is the instantaneous rate of change of magnetic flux with time. (The negative sign is due to Lenz's law.) Where there is more than one turn of conductor in the circuit:

$$E = -N\frac{d\phi}{dt}$$

where N is the number of turns.

The emf generated by a rotating coil is an alternating emf with a sine wave pattern as seen on the oscilloscope.

Peak values

The maximum value shown on the oscilloscope is called the peak value.

Root mean square value

The average value used to represent an alternating voltage is called the root mean square (r.m.s.) value.

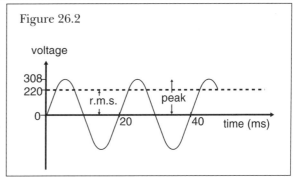

Figure 26.2

The peak value of the voltage V_0 is $\sqrt{2}$ times the root mean square value.

$$V_{\text{rms}} = \frac{V_0}{\sqrt{2}}$$

As the current is directly related to the voltage:

$$I_{\text{rms}} = \frac{I_0}{\sqrt{2}}$$

Problem

The ESB voltage is 220 V (r.m.s. value). What is the peak value of the ESB voltage to your house?

$$\text{peak value} = \sqrt{2}(220) = 308 \text{ V}$$

Transformers change a.c. voltages

A transformer is used to change the voltage of the a.c. supply. It is constructed of separate primary and secondary coils of insulated wire on a laminated soft iron frame. The resistance of the coils is kept low to prevent power losses.

When an alternating voltage is applied across the primary coil it produces an alternating magnetic flux through the primary and soft iron core. This flux cuts through the secondary coil and induces an emf in it.

$$\frac{V_{\text{p}}}{E_{\text{s}}} = \frac{N_{\text{p}}}{N_{\text{s}}}$$

The ratio of secondary turns to primary turns determines whether the transformer is a 'step-up' or 'step-down'.

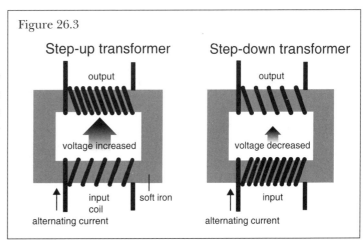

Figure 26.3

Problem 1

A transformer has a primary coil of 200 turns and a secondary coil of 20 turns. The primary coil is connected to a 20 V a.c. supply. What is the emf induced in the secondary coil? Is this a 'step-up' or a 'step-down' transformer?

$$\frac{V_p}{E_s} = \frac{N_p}{N_s}$$

$$\frac{20}{E_s} = \frac{200}{20}$$

$$E_s = 2 \text{ V}$$

It is a 'step-down' transformer.

Problem 2

The coil in the question above is connected the wrong way round and the 20 turns are connected to the 20 V supply. What is the emf induced in the other coil?

20 turns acting as primary coil, 200 turns as secondary.

$$\frac{V_p}{E_s} = \frac{N_p}{N_s}$$

$$\frac{20}{E_s} = \frac{20}{200}$$

$$E_s = 200 \text{ V}$$

This is a dangerous voltage particularly since the expected voltage – as shown above – is only 2 V!

USES OF TRANSFORMERS

The ESB use transformers to 'step up' voltage for transmission of energy and then 'step down' the voltage to supply electrical energy to homes, offices and factories. Transformers are used in TV sets to 'step up' voltage for the tube and also to step down voltage for the electronic circuits. In fact, we use transformers whenever an appliance needs a voltage different from the mains voltage.

MUTUAL INDUCTION

When an emf is generated in the secondary coil by a change in the magnetic field produced by the primary coil, this is **mutual induction.**

SELF-INDUCTION

An emf is generated in a coil by a change in the magnetic field of the same coil, this is **self-induction**.

INDUCTORS AND A.C.

An emf is generated in any coil when the current is changing. These coils have an inductance and are called inductors.

The greater the inductance of the coil, the smaller the current passed by an inductor when connected to a.c.

SUMMARY

- Electromagnetic induction means that an emf is induced whenever the magnetic flux cutting a conductor changes.
- Faraday's law: Whenever there is a change in the magnetic flux cutting a circuit an emf is induced, the strength of which is proportional to the rate of change of flux cutting the circuit.
- Lenz's law: The direction of the induced emf is always such as to oppose the change causing it.
- Right-hand (generator) rule: Put your forefinger, thumb and centre finger of your right hand at right angles to each other. Point your **F**orefinger along the direction of the magnetic **F**ield and your **T**humb along the direction of the **T**hrust (movement). Your **C**entre finger now points along the direction of the induced **C**urrent.
- Mutual induction: where an emf is generated in the secondary coil by a change in the magnetic field produced by the primary coil.
- Self-induction: where an emf is generated in a coil by a change in the magnetic field of the same coil.
- A transformer can step up or step down the voltage of an a.c. (alternating current) supply.
- The greater the inductance of the coil, the smaller the current passed by an inductor when connected to a.c.

Chapter 27 – Applied Electricity: Electromagnetic Induction (Option 2)

THE INDUCTION COIL

The induction coil (invented at Maynooth in 1836 by Nicholas Callan) consists of a primary coil with a make-and-break switch and a secondary coil.

Primary coil

The primary coil has comparatively few turns of thick copper wire.

Secondary coil

The secondary coil consists of many thousands of turns of thin wire wound on top of (but insulated from) the primary. The secondary coil is connected to an adjustable spark gap.

Figure 27.1

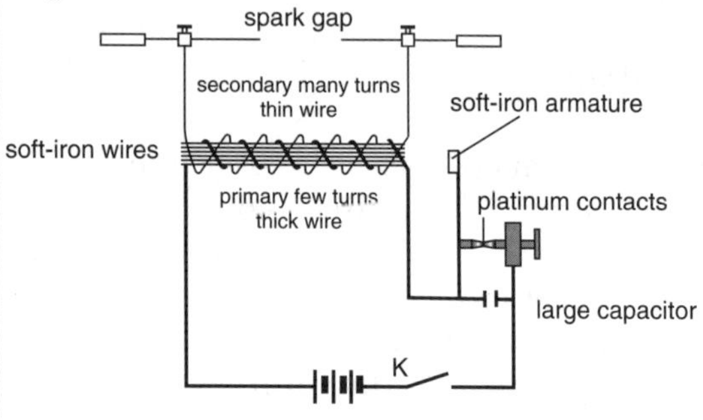

spark gap

secondary many turns thin wire

soft-iron armature

soft-iron wires

primary few turns thick wire

platinum contacts

large capacitor

K

Induction coil

How the induction coil works

When K is closed current flows through the primary coil. The core is now magnetised and attracts the armature that breaks the circuit. The magnetic flux through the primary coil now collapses (the circuit is broken). It also cuts through the secondary coil and induces an emf. The emf induced in the secondary coil is very big and can produce sparks several centimetres long between the points.

What does the capacitor do?

The 'back' emf in the primary coil charges the capacitor. This takes the energy from the circuit so sparking at the contacts is stopped.

USES OF INDUCTION COIL

An induction coil is used in the ignition system of a car and in an electric fence.

THE A.C. GENERATOR

The a.c. generator has a coil of wire (armature) wound on a laminated soft iron core. The magnetic pole pieces are concave and fit closely around the armature. Slip rings are attached to the armature and rotate with it. Carbon brushes press against the slip rings and connect the generator to the outside circuit.

The emf from a generator is increased by: (a) using a strong magnet (or electromagnet); (b) using a laminated soft iron core to produce a large magnetic flux density; (c) using a large number of turns of wire in the armature; (d) increasing the speed of rotation.

As a generator is turned, the induced current flowing through it produces a motor force – this opposes the turning motion. The work done against this force is converted into electrical energy.

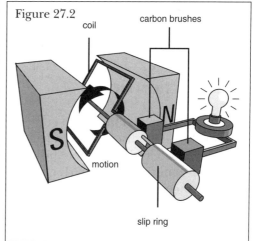

Figure 27.2

INDUCTION EFFECTS IN METALS

When a motor or dynamo moves, the soft iron core of the armature cuts through the magnetic flux. This induces an emf in the core and causes currents (called eddy currents) to flow. If the core is made of one piece the induced currents flow through the resistance of the core material and produce much heat ($H = I^2Rt$). This effect is prevented by making the core of sheets, or laminations, of soft iron that are electrically insulated from each other. The current induced in each separate lamina is small and so the heat loss due to eddy currents is small.

EFFICIENCY OF TRANSFORMERS

If the transformer is 100% efficient.

power of primary circuit = power of secondary coil
$V_P.I_P = V_S.I_S$

An efficient transformer has:

1. Low resistance coils to reduce heating losses.
2. Closely wound primary and secondary coils to ensure that all the magnetic flux links the coils.
3. Laminated core to (a) produce total linkage of magnetic flux and (b) reduce eddy current losses.
4. Core of soft magnetic material to ensure small energy losses in bringing about the constant changes in the magnetic field.

Most transformers have efficiencies in excess of 99%.

SOME PRACTICAL USES OF INDUCTION EFFECTS

The induction furnace, damping in moving coil meters and balances.

THE INDUCTION MOTOR

The rotating magnet induces a current in the copper disc. The disc begins to rotate in the same direction as the magnet and so reduces the relative motion between disc and magnet – the induced current opposes the change causing it.

   This principle is used in a car speedometer.

The simple induction motor

The simple induction motor consists of a rotor which moves and a fixed stator. This is mounted on a free-moving axle. The rotor consists of a cylinder of copper with a core of iron. This is mounted on a shaft and is free to rotate. Around this is fitted a stator. The stator consists of two electromagnets set at right angles to each other and around the rotor. The magnetic field produced by the two electromagnets appears to rotate around the rotor for each complete cycle of the a.c. – in effect, a rotating magnetic flux sweeping round the stator. The rotor attempts to eliminate the relative motion between itself and the rotating magnetic flux by rotating in the same direction. This induces the rotor to spin at the same rate.

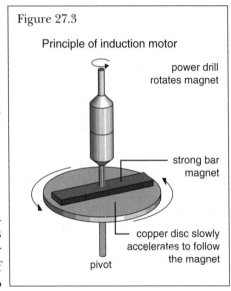

Figure 27.3

Principle of induction motor

power drill rotates magnet

strong bar magnet

copper disc slowly accelerates to follow the magnet

pivot

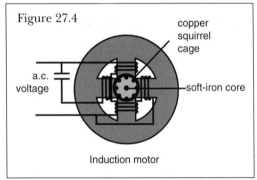

Figure 27.4

copper squirrel cage

a.c. voltage

soft-iron core

Induction motor

SUMMARY

* The induction coil consists of a primary coil with a make-and-break switch and a secondary coil.
* The a.c. generator has slip rings.
* Most transformers have efficiencies in excess of 99%.
* The induction motor uses a rotating magnetic field to produce movement in the rotor.

Chapter 28 – Capacitors and Capacitance

A capacitor is a device for storing a small quantity of electric charge.

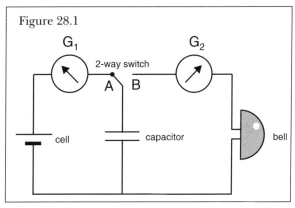

Figure 28.1

When a capacitor is connected to a battery, the current flows to the capacitor for a very short time. Once the capacitor is charged to the same voltage as the battery there is no difference in potential between them – no more current flows.

The charge on a capacitor is directly proportional to the voltage applied.

Capacitance is the ratio of the charge on a capacitor to the potential difference applied across it.

$$C = \frac{Q}{V}$$

Capacitance is measured in farads (F).

Farad (F): A capacitor has a capacitance of one farad when the ratio of charge to potential difference on it is one coulomb per volt.

Problem 1

A parallel plate capacitor is charged to a voltage of 50 V. The charge on the capacitor is 2×10^{-5} C. What is the capacitance of the capacitor?

$$C = \frac{Q}{V}$$
$$= \frac{2 \times 10^{-5}}{50}$$
$$= 0 \cdot 4 \times 10^{-6} \text{ F or } 0 \cdot 4 \text{ } \mu\text{F}$$

Problem 2

A 20 μF capacitor has a charge of $1 \cdot 6 \times 10^{-4}$ C. What is the voltage across the capacitor?

$$C = \frac{Q}{V}$$
$$V = \frac{Q}{C} = \frac{1 \cdot 6 \times 10^{-4}}{20 \times 10^{-6}}$$
$$= 8 \text{ V}$$

Problem 3

A 1 μF capacitor is charged to a voltage of 10 V. What is the charge on each of the plates?

$$C = \frac{Q}{V}$$

$$Q = CV = 1 \times 10^{-6} \times 10 \text{ C}$$

$$= 10^{-5} \text{ C}$$

PARALLEL PLATE CAPACITOR

The simplest form of capacitor consists of a pair of metal plates separated by a thin sheet of insulating material. The insulating material is known as the dielectric.

$$C = \frac{A\varepsilon}{d}$$

Problem 1

A pair of metal plates 0·5 m^2 in area are 0·1 mm apart. Calculate the capacitance when the medium between the plates is air (permittivity of air $\varepsilon = 8\cdot9 \times 10^{-12}$ F m^{-1}).

$$C = \frac{A\varepsilon}{d}$$

$$= \frac{8\cdot9 \times 10^{-12} \times 0\cdot5}{0\cdot1 \times 10^{-3}}$$

$$= 44\cdot5 \times 10^{-9} \text{ F}$$

Problem 2

The capacitance of a parallel plate capacitor is 1·5 μF. The common area of the plates is 0·2 m^2. The material between the plates has a relative permittivity of 5. Calculate the distance between the plates (permittivity of vacuum $\varepsilon_0 = 8\cdot9 \times 10^{-12}$ F m^{-1}).

$$C = \frac{A\varepsilon}{d}$$

$$d = \frac{A\varepsilon}{C}$$

$$= \frac{5(8\cdot9 \times 10^{-12})(0\cdot2)}{1\cdot5 \times 10^{-6}}$$

$$= 5\cdot9 \times 10^{-6} \text{ m}$$

ENERGY STORED IN A CAPACITOR

The energy stored in the capacitor is the energy supplied by the battery to charge the capacitor.

$$W = \frac{1}{2} \cdot CV^2$$

Problem 1

The capacitance of a capacitor is 2·2 μF. When the potential difference between the plates is 10 V. What is the energy stored in the capacitor?

$$W = \frac{1}{2}CV^2$$

$$= \frac{1}{2}(2{\cdot}2 \times 10^{-6})(10)^2$$

$$= 1{\cdot}1 \times 10^{-4}\,\text{J}$$

Problem 2

A capacitor has a capacitance of 4·7 μF. What is the charge on the plates if the energy stored is 0·52 mJ?

$$W = \frac{1}{2}CV^2$$

$$V^2 = \frac{2W}{C} = 2\frac{(0{\cdot}52 \times 10^{-3})}{4{\cdot}7 \times 10^{-6}}$$

$$= 0{\cdot}22 \times 10^3$$

$$= 15\,\text{V}$$

$$Q = CV = 4{\cdot}7 \times 10^{-6}.15 = 70{\cdot}5 \times 10^{-6}\,\text{C}$$

$$= 70{\cdot}5\,\mu\text{C}$$

Capacitors do not conduct in a d.c. circuit

When you connect a capacitor to a battery (direct current – d.c.), the current flows to the capacitor for a very short time. Once the capacitor is charged to the same voltage as the battery there is no difference in potential between them and no more current flows.

There is no continuous flow of current in a capacitor circuit with d.c.

Current flows in a capacitor circuit with a.c.

The larger the capacitance the greater the current flow with a.c.
The greater the frequency the greater the current flow with a.c.

USE OF CAPACITORS

Capacitors are used in a camera flash unit, to filter high-frequency a.c from low-frequency a.c. in hi-fi sound systems, to tune radios and to smooth rectified a.c.

SUMMARY

- A capacitor is a device for storing a small quantity of electric charge.
- Capacitance is the ratio of the charge on a capacitor to the potential difference applied across it.
- Farad: A capacitor has a capacitance of one farad when the ratio of charge to potential difference on it is one coulomb per volt.
- There is no continuous flow of current in a capacitor circuit with d.c.
- In an a.c. circuit the current flow is directly proportional to the capacitance and the frequency of the a.c.

Chapter 29 – Semiconductors

Conductors have loosely bound electrons in their outer electron orbits that are free to move.

Insulators have very tightly bound electrons.

Semiconductors are substances with outer electrons which are not free to move but which require little energy to free them for conduction.

Silicon and germanium are semiconductors.

Intrinsic conduction is the movement of charges through a pure semiconductor.

The intrinsic current is very small and depends on the temperature of the semiconductor.

Extrinsic conduction is the movement of charges through a doped semiconductor.

Doping: the process of adding a small amount of another element to a pure semiconductor to increase its conductivity.

n-type semiconductor: a semiconductor in which electrons are the majority carriers.

p-type semiconductor: a semi-conductor in which 'holes' are the majority carriers.

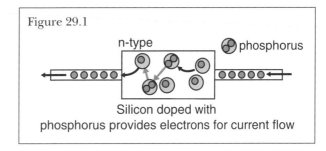

Figure 29.1

n-type   phosphorus

Silicon doped with
phosphorus provides electrons for current flow

MOVEMENT OF HOLES

The movement of 'positive charge' or 'holes' in p-type semiconductors is caused by the movement of electrons in the opposite direction.

Table 29.1

	Majority carriers	**Minority carriers**
n-type	electrons	holes
p-type	holes	electrons

THE DIODE IS A P-N JUNCTION

The diode is formed from a single piece of silicon crystal that is doped by a p-type element on one side and an n-type element on the other.

Unbiased junction

An unbiased p-n junction has a junction area (depletion layer) that has few charges available for conduction and so acts as a barrier to the movement of charges.

Forward-biased junction

This is a p-n junction with the positive terminal of the battery connected to the p-type side and the negative terminal connected to the n-type side. A small voltage (0·6 V for a silicon diode and 0·1 V for a germanium diode) must be applied before any current will flow in a forward-biased junction.

Reverse-biased junction

This has the positive terminal of the battery connected to the n-type material and the negative terminal connected to the p-type material. A reverse-biased p-n junction does not conduct any significant current.

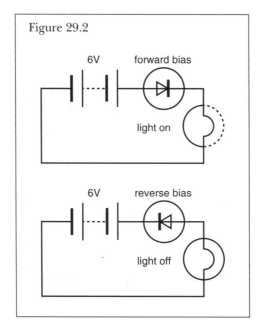

Figure 29.2

THE DIODE IS A HALF-WAVE RECTIFIER

Current flows through a diode only when it is forward-biased so that half of every wave of the a.c. cycle produces a flow of current. The output flows in one direction only and is direct current.

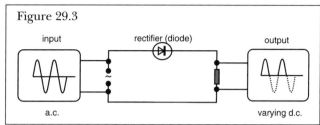

Figure 29.3

LEDs AND PHOTODIODES

The LED (light-emitting diode) gives off light when electricity passes through the p-n junction.

The photodiode is a reverse-biased p-n junction that conducts more electricity when light falls it.

SUMMARY

- Semiconductors are substances with outer electrons which are not free to move but which require little energy to free them for conduction.
- Intrinsic conduction is the movement of charges through a pure semiconductor.
- The intrinsic current is very small and depends on the temperature of the semiconductor.
- Thermal runaway limits the temperature at which germanium semiconductors can be used.
- Doping: the process of adding a small amount of another element to a pure semiconductor to increase its conductivity.
- Extrinsic conduction is the movement of charges through a doped semi-conductor.
- In n-type semiconductors electrons are the main carriers (majority carriers) of electricity.
- In p-type semiconductors the movement of holes is the main conduction process. Holes are the majority carriers of electricity.
- Depletion layer: a p-n junction area that has few charges available for conduction and so acts as a barrier to the movement of charges.
- Diode: A diode is a p-n junction that conducts electricity freely in one direction only.

Chapter 30 – Applied Electricity: Semiconductors (Option 2)

APPLICATIONS OF THE DIODE: RECTIFICATION

When a.c. is connected to a diode, the diode is only forward-biased when the a.c. voltage is positive and current flows through the diode. When the a.c. voltage is negative the diode is reverse-biased and current does not flow. This is half-wave rectification. The output flows in one direction only and so is direct current.

   A rectifier changes a.c. to d.c.

Bridge rectifier: full-wave rectification

A bridge rectifier, or full-wave rectifier, is an arrangement of four diodes. This allows a flow of current for the complete a.c. cycle.

   The addition of a smoothing circuit of an inductor and a capacitor converts the varying d.c. output to smooth d.c.

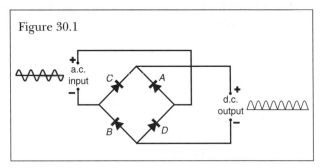

Figure 30.1

LIGHT-EMITTING DIODE (LED)

The LED gives off light when electricity passes through the p-n junction.

   The maximum current an LED can safely pass is very small (about 50 mA) and the forward voltage is about 2·0 V. A series resistor is required to keep the current below the maximum value.

Uses of LEDs

LEDs are used as current on/off indicators, as the numerical display in calculators and as part of an optical switch. The LED is better than filament bulbs for these displays because of: (a) small size, (b) very small current required to operate them, (c) they have a long life and (d) they operate at a fast speed.

PHOTODIODE

The photodiode is a p-n junction with a 'window' that exposes the junction to light. The photodiode is operated in reverse bias. When light energy falls on the junction, electrons and 'holes' are produced in the semiconductor. This increases the current in proportion to the intensity of the light falling on it.

Optical switch

This consists of an LED and a photodiode. When current flows through the LED it emits light. The light falls on the photodiode. Current flows through the photodiode and completes the circuit.

Optical switches have many applications. They are used as safety guards in machines, end-of-tape indicators in tape recorders, out-of-paper controls in printers and as a smoke alarms.

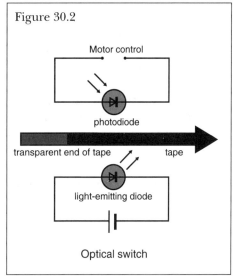

Figure 30.2

TRANSISTOR

Bipolar transistor

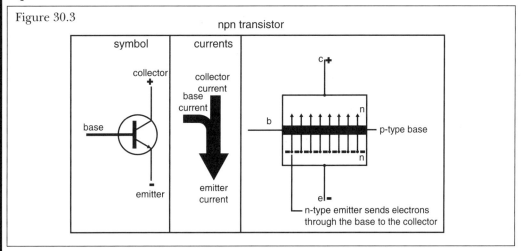

Figure 30.3

The npn bipolar transistor is a sandwich containing a thin slice of p-type material between two much thicker slices of n-type material. Transistors are usually made in a number of steps from a single piece of semiconductor. The thin centre slice of material is known as the **base** and the other two slices as the **emitter** and the **collector**. The emitter is usually more heavily 'doped' than the other two parts.

There are two p-n junctions in the transistor.

The transistor operates with:

(a) the emitter-base junction forward-biased
(b) the base-collector junction reverse-biased.

How the transistor works

Once the voltage across the forward-biased emitter-base junction is greater than 0·6 V, electrons flow from the emitter into the base. Since the base is very thin the electrons do not have to go very far to be attracted by the positive voltage on the collector. In this way most of the electrons flowing from the emitter reach the collector (even though the base-collector junction is negatively biased). About 99% of the electrons flowing from the emitter to the base reach the collector. Once the emitter-base voltage falls below 0·6 V the current is cut off.

Clearly the transistor can be switched on and off by the base voltage.
The base voltage controls the base current which in turn controls the collector current. $I_e = I_c + I_b$
The amplification factor or 'gain' of the transistor is k.

$$I_c = k\, I_b$$

Switching action of the transistor

The light sensor switch demonstrates the switching action of the transistor.

Reason for a reverse-biased diode in relay circuits

A reverse-biased diode is used in transistor circuits that contain electromagnetic relays. This is because of the self-inductance of the relay coil. When the relay is switched on (or off) a high voltage is induced across the coil. This would destroy the transistor. The diode

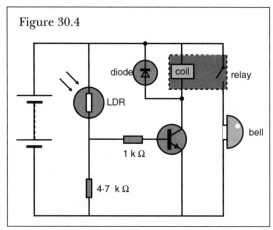

Figure 30.4

offers a low resistance path to this voltage and protects the transistor.

Temperature sensor or fire alarm

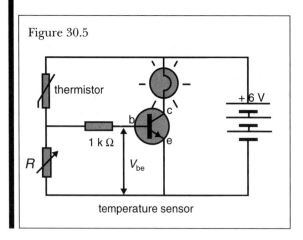

Figure 30.5

temperature sensor

pnp transistors

A pnp transistor is similar in construction and operation to the npn. In the pnp transistor a thin slice of n-type semiconductor is sandwiched between pieces of p-type material.

THE TRANSISTOR IS A VOLTAGE AMPLIFIER

The transistor is used as a voltage amplifier to produce an enlarged copy of an alternating voltage input.

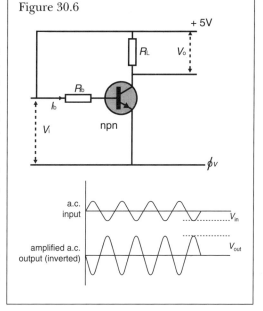

Figure 30.6

Bias resistor

In practical transistor circuits just one power supply is provided. The transistor is connected so that the base-emitter junction is forward-biased and the base-collector circuit is reverse-biased. This is done by connecting a base bias resistor R_b in the circuit as shown in Figure 30.6.

The bias resistor is a large series resistor which limits the base current I_b to a safe value.

Load resistor

The voltage across the load resistor – by Ohm's law $V = I_c \times R_L$ – is the output voltage.

THE TRANSISTOR IS A VOLTAGE INVERTER

A voltage inverter always gives an output voltage that is the opposite of the input voltage. We use the same basic circuit as in the voltage amplifier but we take the output across the transistor (the collector-emitter voltage V_{ce}).

The action of the transistor as a voltage amplifier or as a voltage inverter depends on whether you take the output across a load resistor or across the transistor.

LOGIC GATES

A logic gate is a device that gives an output signal only when certain conditions are met in the input signal.

AND gate: a circuit where there is an output only when BOTH inputs are ON.

OR gate: a circuit where there is an output when EITHER input is ON.

All the sorting, processing, control and other functions in digital computers are carried out by semiconductor logic gates built into the integrated circuits.

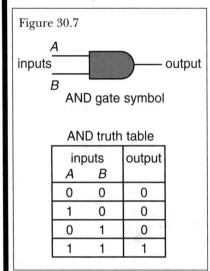

Figure 30.7

AND gate symbol

inputs — output

A

B

AND truth table

inputs		output
A	B	
0	0	0
1	0	0
0	1	0
1	1	1

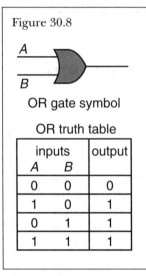

Figure 30.8

OR gate symbol

A

B

OR truth table

inputs		output
A	B	
0	0	0
1	0	1
0	1	1
1	1	1

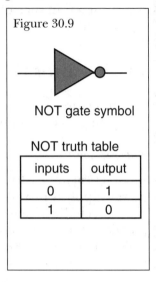

Figure 30.9

NOT gate symbol

NOT truth table

inputs	output
0	1
1	0

NOT gate: a circuit where there is an output only when the input is OFF.
    The voltage inverter acts as a NOT gate. When the input is high the output is low and when the input is low the output is high.

AND, OR and **NOT** gates are in practice made as integrated circuits (ICs) with connections for inputs, power supply and output.

SUMMARY

- A rectifier changes a.c. to d.c.
- A light-emitting diode emits light when current flows through it.
- Photodiode: the current flowing through a p-n junction operated in reverse bias increases when light falls on the junction.
- The base voltage controls the base current, that in turn controls the collector current.
- A reverse-biased diode is used in relay circuits because of the self-inductance of the relay. The diode offers a low resistance path to the resultant current.
- The action of a transistor as a voltage amplifier or as a voltage inverter, depends on whether you take the output across a load resistor or across the transistor.
- AND gate: a circuit where there is an output only when BOTH inputs are ON.
- OR gate: a circuit where there is an output when EITHER input is ON.
- NOT gate: a circuit where there is an output only when the input is OFF.
- AND, OR and NOT gates are in practice made as integrated circuits (ICs) with connections for inputs, power supply and output.

Chapter 31 – The Electron

In 1895, J.B. Perrin showed that cathode rays have a negative electric charge.

Electrons have a negative charge

In 1897, J.J. Thomson found that electrons are deflected by a magnetic field in a way that shows they are a beam of negative charge. He also deflected electrons with an electric field.

The electron beam was deflected by a fixed amount by a magnetic field (and by the electric field). This means that **all electrons have the same mass and electric charge.**

Experiments show that electrons (cathode rays):

1. cause fluorescence
2. affect photographic plates
3. travel in straight lines
4. are deflected by magnetic and electric fields in a direction which shows them to be negative
5. cause a heating effect when they strike a small target
6. can pass through a thin metal foil
7. produce X-rays when they strike a heavy metal target
8. have a nature that is independent of the metal used in the cathode.

The idea that there was a natural unit of electricity in each atom was suggested in 1891 by George Johnstone Stoney (1826–1911) of Galway. Stoney named the unit an electron.

Energy of an electron

An electron accelerated across a potential difference of 1 volt has an energy of **one electron-volt** or **1 eV.** When the voltage is 1,000 V the energy is **1 keV**. A MeV is 10^6 **eV** and a **GeV** is 10^9 **eV.**

The charge of the electron

Thomson measured the ratio of the electric charge of the electron to the mass of the electron in 1897. He found that the specific charge (charge to mass ratio) of the electron did not vary.

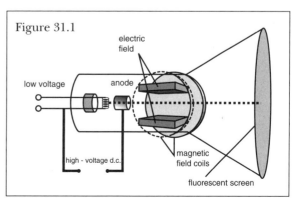

Figure 31.1

An electron is a particle found in all matter that carries the fundamental unit of negative charge.

Millikan measured the charge of the electron in 1909. The smallest charge measured by Millikan was 1.6×10^{-19} C and every other charge was a whole number multiple of this charge. He concluded from this and from other evidence that the charge of the electron is 1.6×10^{-19} C.

THE MASS OF THE ELECTRON

The value of $\frac{e}{m}$ is 1.76×10^{11} C kg^{-1} from Thomson's experiment. The charge of the electron is 1.6×10^{-19} C (from Millikan). We can calculate the mass of the electron from these values.

$$\frac{e}{m} = 1.76 \times 10^{11}$$

$$e = 1.6 \times 10^{-19}$$

$$m = 9.09 \times 10^{-31} \text{ kg}$$

The mass of the hydrogen atom is about 2,000 times the mass of the electron.

Problem

An electron beam in a cathode ray tube carries a current of 10 mA. Calculate the number of electrons crossing the tube each second.

$$10 \text{ mA} = 10 \times 10^{-3} \text{ C s}^{-1}$$

$$1 \text{ e} = 1.6 \times 10^{-19} \text{ C}$$

$$\text{Number of electrons} = \frac{10 \times 10^{-3}}{1.6 \times 10^{-19}} = 6.25 \times 10^{16}$$

THERMIONIC EMISSION

Thermionic emission is the emission of electrons from a hot metal surface.

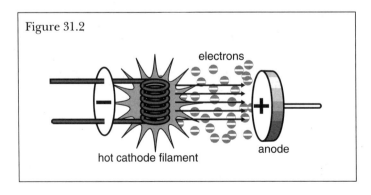

Figure 31.2

electrons

hot cathode filament

anode

1. Electrons are emitted from the surface of a hot metal.
2. The higher the temperature of the metal the more electrons are emitted.
3. Electrons are accelerated across the vacuum only when the anode is at a positive potential.
4. The greater the positive potential of the anode the greater the current up to a limit – the saturation current.

Work function is the minimum amount of energy necessary to release an electron from the surface of a metal.

HOW THE CATHODE RAY TUBE PRODUCES A PICTURE

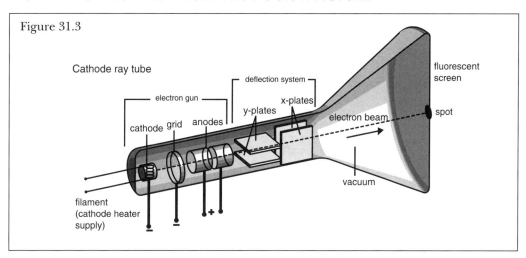

Figure 31.3

USES OF THERMIONIC EMISSION

Oscilloscope

An oscilloscope is a cathode ray tube used to measure a.c. frequencies and voltages. Vertical and horizontal plates deflect the electron beam. A voltage across the Y-plates produces a deflection of the beam proportional to the voltage. A voltage is applied to the X-plates that deflects the beam steadily across the screen and then jumps back rapidly. This is the time-base circuit and can be varied from microseconds to about 10 seconds. A combination of the two deflections produces the oscilloscope trace.

Electrocardiograph (ECG) and electroencephalograph (EEG)

A cathode ray oscilloscope is used to display the signal trace in an electrocardiograph that monitors the electrical activity of the heart.

The electrical activity of the brain can be measured with an electroencephalograph.

Television

A television set is a cathode ray tube. An electron beam sweeps across the screen, flies back very quickly (so fast you don't even see it) and sweeps across again lower down so that a complete picture is produced by the beam moving down the screen.

Colour television

The screen is made of carefully placed lines of three different phosphors. These produce red, green or blue light when struck by an electron beam. Three electron guns produce electron beams – one for each colour phosphor. Combinations of the three primary colours produced by the phosphors give all other colours.

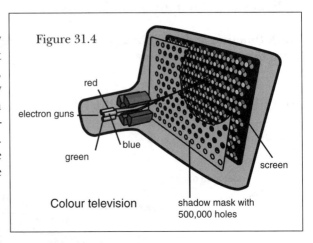

Figure 31.4

SUMMARY

- Cathode rays are electrons.
- Cathode rays travel in straight lines, cause fluorescence, affect photographic plates, are deflected by magnetic and electric fields, cause heating when they strike a target, can pass through thin metal foil and can produce X-rays.
- An electron is a particle which carries the fundamental unit of negative charge and is found in all matter.
- Thermionic emission is the emission of electrons from a hot metal surface.
- Work function is the minimum amount of energy necessary to release an electron from the surface of a metal.

Chapter 32 – Photoelectric Emission and X-rays

Hallwachs found that negative charges were emitted by the zinc plate when UV light shone on it. Hallwachs' experiments were the result of a discovery by Hertz that the distance a spark could jump was increased if ultraviolet light fell on the gap.

Thomson found the charge to mass ratio of the negative charges released in photoelectric emission was identical to electrons. As the electrons are freed from the metal by light we refer to them as 'photoelectrons'.

Experiments on the photoelectric effect showed:

1. that electrons are emitted when light of suitable frequency falls on a metal surface,
2. below a certain frequency of light (the threshold frequency) no electrons are emitted regardless of the intensity of the light,
3. the number of electrons emitted depends on the intensity of the light,
4. the energy of the electrons emitted depends on the frequency of the light.

Photoelectric effect: The emission of electrons from the surface of a metal when electromagnetic radiation of suitable frequency falls on it.

The threshold frequency is the minimum frequency of light necessary to cause photoelectric emission.

Photoelectric emission could not be explained by the wave theory of light.

PLANCK'S QUANTUM THEORY

Planck put forward his theory in 1900. He said that light (and other electromagnetic energy) is emitted and absorbed in a small 'packet' or quantum. Each quantum contains a definite amount of energy that depends only on the frequency of the light.

The quantum of energy is given by the equation

$$E = hf$$

where h is a constant – called Planck's constant.

Problem

Calculate the number of photons emitted per second by a 100 W bulb if the wavelength emitted is 600 nm. Assume 10% of the energy of the bulb is emitted as light.

Energy of one photon:

$$E = hf = \frac{hc}{\lambda}$$

$$= 6 \cdot 6 \times 10^{-34} \cdot \frac{3 \times 10^8}{600 \times 10^{-9}}$$

$$= 0 \cdot 33 \times 10^{-17} \, \text{J}$$

10% of 100 W = 10 W = 10 J s^{-1}

number of photons per second $n = \dfrac{10}{0 \cdot 33 \times 10^{-17}}$

$$= 3 \cdot 03 \times 10^{18} \text{ photons}$$

EINSTEIN'S PHOTOELECTRIC LAW

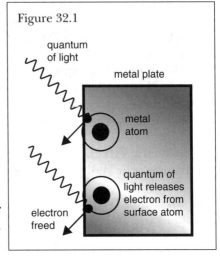

Figure 32.1

1. Each quantum of light travels closely concentrated in space. A quantum of light energy is called a photon.
2. In photoelectric emission a photon gives up all its energy to one electron.

A photon is a quantum of light energy whose energy is given by Planck's equation $E = hf$

The work function is the minimum amount of energy necessary to release an electron from the surface of a metal.

When a photon has an energy hf, greater than the work function Φ, the remainder of the photon energy $(hf - \Phi)$ is the maximum amount of kinetic energy the electron can have.

Einstein's Photoelectric law:

$$hf = \Phi + \frac{1}{2} mv^2_{\text{max}}$$

A photon has wave properties in that its energy depends on the frequency and also particle properties by being closely confined in space and by interacting with matter as a single unit.

The threshold frequency (f_0) is the minimum frequency of light necessary to cause photoelectric emission.

Problem 1

Calculate the energy of a 900 nm photon.

$$E = hf = \frac{hc}{\lambda} = 6 \cdot 6 \times 10^{-34} \cdot \frac{3 \cdot 0 \times 10^8}{900 \times 10^{-19}} = 2 \cdot 2 \times 10^{-19} \, \text{J}$$

Problem 2

A metal has a work function of 1·0 eV. Calculate the maximum kinetic energy of electrons emitted when this metal is illuminated by light of wavelength 900 nm.

energy of 900 nm photon = $2 \cdot 2 \times 10^{-19}$ J (from above)

work function = $1 \cdot 0$ eV = $1 \cdot 0 \times 1 \cdot 6 \times 10^{-19}$ J = $1 \cdot 6 \times 10^{-19}$ J

Einstein's photoelectric law:

$(\frac{1}{2} mv^2) \max = hf - \Phi$

$= (2 \cdot 2 \times 10^{-19}) - (1 \cdot 6 \times 10^{-19})$

$= 0 \cdot 6 \times 10^{-19}$ J

PHOTOCELL

A photocell is a vacuum tube with a concave cathode made from a material that emits photoelectrons easily. Photoelectrons are emitted when light above the threshold frequency falls on it.

Uses of photocell

Photocells are used in burglar alarms, smoke alarms, automatic doors, safety switches on cutting machinery, laboratory light meters, optical soundtrack in film and control sensors in central heating boilers.

Solid state photodiodes, photoresistors, light-dependent resistors (LDRs) and phototransistors have replaced the photocell in many of these uses.

X-RAYS

Roentgen discovered X-rays in 1895. X-rays were found to have the following properties:

1. X-rays are produced when fast electrons strike a solid body.
2. X-rays produce fluorescence.
3. X-rays blacken photographic emulsions. Roentgen took the first radiograph of his wife's hand.
4. X-rays cannot be deflected by electric and magnetic fields.
5. X-rays travel in straight lines and cannot be reflected or refracted easily.
6. X-rays cause ionisation of the air.
7. X-rays are diffracted by thin crystals.
8. X-rays penetrate most substances.
9. X-rays are absorbed by materials depending on the thickness and the density of the substance.
10. X-rays are electromagnetic radiation of extremely short wavelength. X-rays have wavelengths from 10^{-9} to 10^{-15} m.

X-rays are electromagnetic radiation of extremely short wavelength.

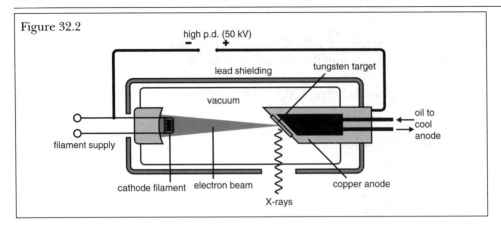

Figure 32.2

HOT-CATHODE X-RAY TUBE

1. The hot-cathode X-ray tube has a hot cathode that produces electrons by thermionic emission.
2. A vacuum ensures that nothing slows the electrons.
3. A tungsten target is set into the anode.
4. The high voltage (>50 kV) across the tube accelerates the electrons.
5. The high-energy electrons hit the tungsten target in the anode and produce X-rays.
6. Only 1% of the electrons produce X-rays.
7. About 99% of the electrons produce heat in the anode. The heat produced is dissipated by cooling fins or cooling liquids circulated through the anode.
8. A lead shield with a small window ensures that X-rays are emitted in one direction.

X-ray intensity depends on the temperature of the cathode.

X-ray penetrating power depends on voltage across the tube.

X-rays are emitted when an electron falls from an outer electron orbit (high energy level) to an inner orbit (lower energy). This happens when a fast electron knocks an electron out of an inner orbit. An electron from an outer orbit falls into this vacant place. The energy given off is an X-ray.

X-ray production is the inverse process of photoelectric emission. In photoelectric emission photon energy frees an electron. In X-ray emission the electron energy frees an X-ray photon.

Problem

Calculate the wavelength of the X-ray photons emitted when electrons accelerated across a tube at a potential of 50 kV strike a tungsten target.

Energy of the electrons: $eV = (1 \cdot 6 \times 10^{-19}) \, (50 \times 10^{3}) = 80 \times 10^{-16}$

Energy of photon produced: $E = hf$

$$f = \frac{E}{h} = \frac{80 \times 10^{-16}}{6.6 \times 10^{-34}} = 1.212 \times 10^{19} \, \text{Hz}$$

$$\lambda = \frac{c}{f} = \frac{3 \times 10^8}{1.212 \times 10^{19}} = 2.475 \times 10^{-11} \, \text{m}$$

DETECTION OF X-RAYS

X-rays are detected by fluorescence in some materials and by a blackening of photographic film.

USES OF X-RAYS

X-rays are used to diagnose and locate breaks in bones. CAT scans form images from a number of X-ray 'slices' through the body. Very penetrating X-rays are used in X-ray therapy to destroy cancer cells.

X-rays are used to check welds in pressure vessels and in aircraft bodies as well as detecting cracks in machinery under stress. X-rays are used in security checks of baggage in airports.

Research scientists use X-ray diffraction to discover the structure of crystals and large molecules.

Harmful effects of X-rays

X-rays have the same harmful effects as other ionising radiation (radioactive substances). Radiographers wear lead-lined aprons and stand behind lead glass screens to prevent radiation damage.

SUMMARY

- Photoelectric effect: the emission of electrons from the surface of a metal when electromagnetic radiation of suitable frequency falls on it.
- Photon: a packet of electromagnetic (light) energy whose energy is given by Planck's equation $E = hf$.
- Work function is the minimum amount of energy necessary to release an electron from the surface of a metal.
- Threshold frequency is the minimum frequency of light necessary to cause photoelectric emission.
- Einstein's photoelectric equation: $hf = \Phi + \frac{1}{2} mv^2_{max}$

- X-rays are produced when fast electrons strike a solid metal target.
- X-rays are electromagnetic radiation of extremely short wavelength.
- X-rays cause ionisation of the air and other materials.
- X-rays penetrate most materials.

Chapter 33 – Radioactivity

Becquerel discovered that uranium salts produced a type of penetrating radiation. The Curies chemically separated substances that produce penetrating radiation naturally. Polonium, Thorium and Radium are some radioactive elements.

Natural radioactivity is the spontaneous disintegration of the nucleus with the emission of alpha (α), beta (β) or gamma (γ) radiation.

A diffusion cloud chamber shows ionisation and penetration.

Penetrating power increases:
$\alpha \qquad \beta \qquad \gamma$
$\Rightarrow$

Ionising power increases:
$\gamma \qquad \beta \qquad \alpha$
$\Rightarrow$

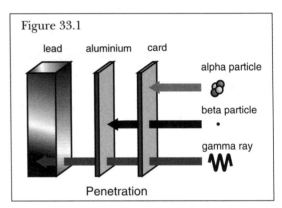

Figure 33.1

lead   aluminium   card

alpha particle

beta particle

gamma ray

Penetration

ALPHA PARTICLES ARE HELIUM NUCLEI

Properties of alpha particles

1. Cause fluorescence.
2. Blacken photographic plates.
3. Are strongly ionising – producing 10,000 pairs of ions per cm of air travelled.
4. Have weak penetration – are stopped by paper or 5 cm of air.
5. Have an electric charge of +2 (or $+3 \cdot 2 \times 10^{-19}$ C)
6. Have an atomic mass of 4 a.m.u.
7. Have velocities ranging from $0 \cdot 5\%$ to 1% of the speed of light.
8. Are identical to doubly ionised helium atoms.

An α particle is a combination of two protons and two neutrons ejected from the nucleus.

The emission of an α particle from the nucleus takes two protons and two neutrons from the nucleus. This leaves a nucleus with an atomic number two less and an atomic mass four less.

$$^{228}_{90}\text{Th} \Rightarrow {}^{224}_{88}\text{Ra} + {}^{4}_{2}\text{He } (\alpha)$$

BETA PARTICLES ARE HIGH-SPEED ELECTRONS

Properties of beta particles

1. Cause fluorescence.
2. Blacken photographic plates.
3. Are moderately ionising – producing about 100 pairs of ions per cm of air travelled.
4. Moderately penetrating – are stopped by about 500 cm of air.
5. Have an electric charge of -1 $(-1.6 \times 10^{-19}$ C).
6. Have the same mass (when at rest) as the electron.
7. Have velocities ranging from 30% to 70% of the speed of light.
8. Are high-speed electrons originating in the nucleus.

A β particle is a high-speed electron ejected by the decay in the nucleus of a neutron into a proton.

$$^{212}_{82}\text{Pb} \Rightarrow \, ^{212}_{83}\text{Bi} + \beta$$

As the sum of the atomic numbers and of the mass numbers on each side must be equal, the β particle is written as $^{0}_{-1}\text{e}$:

$$^{212}_{82}\text{Pb} \Rightarrow \, ^{212}_{83}\text{Bi} + \, ^{0}_{-1}\text{e}$$

GAMMA RAYS ARE ELECTROMAGNETIC RADIATION OF EXTREMELY SHORT WAVELENGTH

When a nucleus emits a γ ray photon the structure of the nucleus does not change.

Properties of gamma rays

1. Cause slight fluorescence.
2. Blacken photographic plates.
3. Are only weakly ionising.
4. Are very penetrating, passing through a considerable thickness of material.
5. Have no electric charge – are not deflected by electric or magnetic fields.
6. Have zero mass.
7. Have the same velocity as light.
8. Can be diffracted.
9. Produce a photoelectric effect.
10. Are shown by measurements to have shorter wavelengths than X-rays.

Problem

How many α particles and β particles are emitted from the following radioactive decay?

$$^{235}_{92}\text{U} \Rightarrow \, ^{207}_{82}\text{Pb}$$

Table 33.1

	Atomic number	Atomic mass
α particles	decrease by 2	decrease by 4
β particles	increase by 1	no change

Mass change is $235 - 207 = 28$
Number of α particles $= \dfrac{28}{4} = 7$

Seven α particles decreases atomic number by $14(7 \times 2)$
Atomic number should be $= 92 - 14 = 78$
Atomic number is in fact $82 =$ increased by $4 =$ four β particles emitted.
Answer: Seven α particles and four β particles.

HOW TO DETECT RADIATION

Geiger-Müller tube

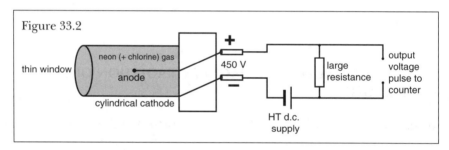

Figure 33.2

The principle of the Geiger-Müller (G-M) tube is that radiation ionises the gas in the tube and produces an electric current. The G-M tube consists of a central thin wire anode and a cylindrical cathode maintained at a potential difference of 500 V. The tube contains a monatomic gas (neon) at low pressure.

A Geiger-Müller tube and electronic counter is called a Geiger counter.

Solid-state detector

A solid-state detector consists of a diode – a 'p–n' in 'reverse bias'. When radiation passes through the diode it 'knocks out' electrons, produces more charge carriers and a pulse of electricity flows. The solid-state detector can

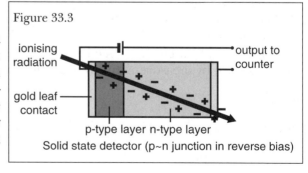

Figure 33.3

Solid state detector (p~n junction in reverse bias)

detect very low energy particles and can also distinguish between different types of radiation.

A solid-state detector is a 'p–n' junction in 'reverse bias'.

SUMMARY

- Natural radioactivity is the spontaneous disintegration of the nucleus with the emission of alpha, beta or gamma radiation.

Table 33.2

	Nature	Charge	Ionising power	Penetrating power
α **particle**	two protons and two neutrons (helium nucleus)	+2	good	poor
β **particle**	high-speed electron	−1	medium	medium
γ **ray**	electromagnetic radiation of very short wavelength ($<10^{-15}$ m)	0	poor	good

- Principle of Geiger-Müller tube: Radiation ionises the gas in the chamber. A strong electric field accelerates electrons and produces an 'avalanche' effect of further ionisation that produces a large number of electrons. This current produces a voltage pulse across a resistor that is detected by the counter.
- Principle of solid-state detector: Radiation striking a reverse biased p–n junction causes a greater current to flow.

Chapter 34 – The Structure of the Atom

RUTHERFORD'S GOLD FOIL EXPERIMENT

Rutherford put forward a model of the atom that has all the positive charge concentrated in a very small volume – the nucleus.

The nucleus has a radius of the order of 10^{-15} m. The size of the atom – the space occupied by the electrons – is much greater. The radius of the atom is of the order of 10^{-10} m. If you picture the nucleus as a football the atom is the size of the stadium!

The nucleus has a radius of the order of 10^{-15} m
The atom has a radius of the order of 10^{-10} m

Rutherford discovered the proton in 1919

Rutherford proved that when an alpha particle bombards a nitrogen nucleus it is changed (transmuted) to oxygen and that a proton was given off in the nuclear reaction.

$$^4_2He + ^{14}_7N \Rightarrow ^{17}_8O + ^1_1H$$

Chadwick discovered the neutron in 1932

Chadwick showed that the radiation emitted when an alpha particle strikes a beryllium nucleus was due to a particle with a mass close to that of the proton but with no electric charge – the neutron.

$$^9_4Be + ^4_2He \Rightarrow ^{12}_6C + ^1_0n$$

The nucleus is composed of protons and neutrons.

Atomic number of an element (Z): The number of protons in the nucleus of the atom of the element. It is also the number of electrons around the nucleus of a neutral atom of the element.

Isotopes: Atoms of the same atomic number (of the same element – same number of protons) but with a different atomic mass (different number of neutrons).

The most common isotope of carbon is used as the standard to compare the masses of different isotopes. An atom of this isotope of carbon is taken as having a mass of 12 atomic mass units.

Relative atomic mass: The mass of an atom in atomic mass units, where the mass of the carbon-12 isotope is taken as having a mass of 12 units.

Mass number (A): This is the whole number nearest to the relative atomic mass of an atom. It gives the number of protons and neutrons in the nucleus.

Lasers

A laser tube produces a beam of light in which all the waves are of the same frequency and in phase. As a result of constructive interference a beam of high-energy light is produced. This narrow beam can be controlled with great precision.

THE BOHR MODEL OF THE ATOM

1. Electrons can exist only in certain definite orbits, or energy levels, around the nucleus. As long as they are in these orbits they do not lose energy.
2. When an electron jumps from one energy level to another it emits the energy in a photon. Planck's equation gives the wavelength: $E_2 - E_1 = hf$.

An emission spectrum is a spectrum given out by a substance when its atoms are excited.

Line spectra are explained by the Bohr model as the wavelengths emitted when an electron jumps from one energy level to another.

Problem

An electron jumps from an electron energy level of 0·0045 to one of 0·0030 eV. Calculate the frequency of the emitted photon.

$$E_2 - E_1 = hf$$

$$E_2 - E_1 = 0{\cdot}0045 - 0{\cdot}0030 \text{ eV} = 0{\cdot}0015 \times 1{\cdot}6 \times 10^{-19} \text{ J} = 2{\cdot}4 \times 10^{-22}$$

$$E_2 - E_1 = hf$$

$$f = \frac{E_2 - E_1}{h} = \frac{2{\cdot}4 \times 10^{-22}}{6{\cdot}6 \times 10^{-34}}$$

$$= 0{\cdot}36 \times 10^{12} \text{ Hz} = 3{\cdot}6 \times 10^{11} \text{ Hz}$$

SUMMARY

- Atomic number of an element (Z): the number of protons in the nucleus of the atom of the element. It is also the number of electrons around the nucleus of the neutral atom.
- Relative atomic mass: the mass of the atom in atomic mass units where the mass of the carbon-12 isotope is taken as having a mass of 12.
- Isotope: atoms of the same atomic number but with a different atomic mass. Isotopes have the same number of protons but different numbers of neutrons.
- Mass number (A): the whole number nearest the relative atomic mass of an element. It equals the number of protons and neutrons in the nucleus.

Chapter 35 – Radioactive Decay

The rate at which radiation is emitted from a given substance depends only on the amount of the substance present (the number of atoms of the radioactive substance).

Law of radioactive decay: The rate of radioactive decay depends only on number of atoms of radioactive substance present.

Rate of decay = $-\lambda N$

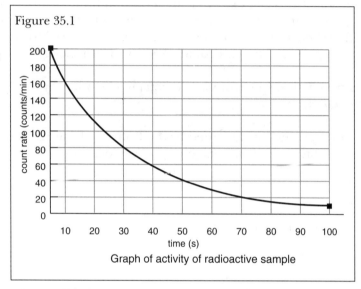

Figure 35.1

Graph of activity of radioactive sample

Where λ is the decay constant (the negative sign indicates that it is a 'decay' process) and N is the number of atoms in the sample.

The rate of decay is the number of nuclear disintegrations occurring per second.

The becquerel (Bq) is a rate of decay of one disintegration per second.

The half-life ($T_{\frac{1}{2}}$) is the time taken for half the number of atoms of a radioactive substance to decay.

Half-life and decay constant

A substance with a short half-life decays very fast and has a big decay constant.

A substance with a long half-life decays very slowly and has a small decay constant.

Decay constant and half-life are inversely related.

$$T_{\frac{1}{2}} = \frac{\ln 2}{\lambda}$$

$$T_{\frac{1}{2}} = \frac{0.693}{\lambda}$$

Problem 1

A radioactive substance has a half-life of 2·4 days. Calculate the time taken for a radioactive sample to decay to one-sixteenth of the original activity.

One half-life $\Rightarrow \frac{1}{2}$ activity

Two half-lives $\Rightarrow \frac{1}{4}$ activity

Three half-lives $\Rightarrow \frac{1}{8}$ activity

Four half-lives $\Rightarrow \frac{1}{16}$ activity

Four half-lives $= 4 \times 2\cdot4$ days $= 9\cdot6$ days

Problem 2

The decay constant for a particular radioactive isotope is $3\cdot5 \times 10^4$ s^{-1}. Calculate its half-life. Comment on the result.

$$T_{\frac{1}{2}} = 0\cdot693/\lambda$$
$$= \frac{0\cdot693}{3\cdot5 \times 10^4}$$
$$= 0\cdot198 \times 10^{-4}$$
$$= 1\cdot98 \times 10^{-5} \text{ s}$$

The decay constant is very big so the half-life must be very short.

Nuclear reactions

1. Conservation of electric charge: this requires that the sum of the atomic numbers of the initial nuclei must equal the sum of the atomic numbers of the resultant nuclei.
2. Conservation of mass–energy: Energy is conserved in any individual reaction, provided that mass is taken as a form of energy according to the equation $E = mc^2$.
3. Conservation of momentum: the momentum before the reaction equals the momentum after.
4. The total number of nucleons also remains unchanged.

SUMMARY

- Law of radioactive decay: The rate of decay is proportional to the number of atoms of the radioactive substance present.
- A becquerel (Bq): this is a rate of decay of one disintegration per second.
- Half-life: the time taken for half the number of atoms of a radioactive substance to disintegrate. The half-life is a constant and is related only to the decay constant.

Chapter 36 – Uses of Radioisotopes and Radiation Hazards

Natural radioactivity is radioactivity produced by substances found in nature – substances like uranium, radium and thorium.

Artificial radioactivity: radioactivity produced by bombarding non-radioactive isotopes with charged particles or neutrons.

Radioactive isotopes have many uses in medicine, agriculture, research and industry.

MEDICAL USES OF RADIOISOTOPES

Radioisotopes are used:

1. like X-rays to produce photographic images of the inside of the body,
2. to kill cancerous cells,
3. to sterilise prepacked syringes, scalpels, bandages and dressings as well as heat-sensitive medicines. Exposing substances to γ radiation does not make them radioactive.

Injections of salt containing the radioisotope sodium–24 into the bloodstream enable doctors to chart the flow of blood through the body.

Plutonium–238 radioisotope is used to generate electricity to power heart pacemakers.

INDUSTRIAL USES OF RADIOISOTOPES

Smoke detectors.

Radioisotope generators power satellites and warning beacons at sea.

Gamma-ray photography is used to check jet engines, aircraft frames and pipelines.

Gamma rays are used to check the thickness of materials.

Radioisotope tracers are used to check pipes for leaks.

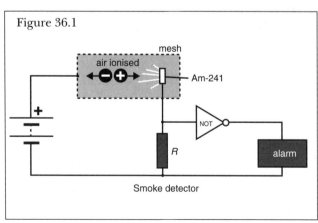

Figure 36.1

mesh

air ionised

Am-241

NOT

R

alarm

Smoke detector

AGRICULTURAL USES OF RADIOISOTOPES

Very high levels of γ radiation are used to sterilise foods.

The radioisotope phosphorus–32 (in a phosphate fertiliser) is used in agricultural research to monitor the intake of phosphates by plants.

Another use is in treating male insect pests with γ radiation – this makes them sterile.

RESEARCH USES OF RADIOISOTOPES

Radioactive isotopes decay at a known rate and so can be used to determine the age of things.

Carbon dating uses the relative amounts of radioactive carbon–14 to carbon–12 to give a measure of the age of a dead plant or animal sample.

Uranium–238 dating uses the relative amounts of uranium–238 and lead–206 to date the age of the rock.

Radioactivation analysis

When a tiny sample of a substance is bombarded with neutrons it turns into radioactive isotopes of the same elements. The half-lives of these isotopes and the wavelengths of the gamma rays emitted enable scientists to identify the substances.

EFFECTS OF IONISING RADIATION ON YOUR HEALTH

Alpha particle radiation

Alpha radiation is stopped by the layer of dead cells above the live skin tissue. Alpha radiation is very dangerous if alpha emitters are taken into live tissue in a skin cut or breathed into the lungs in dust, liquid or gas. This is because it is a strongly ionising radiation and this causes great damage to cells.

Beta particle radiation

Beta particles can penetrate about 1 cm of body tissue. Beta emitters endanger skin tissue but do not affect the deeper organs of the body unless taken in through dust, liquids or gas.

Gamma radiation and X-rays

Both of these radiations can penetrate right through the body and so endanger all parts of the body. Gamma emitters are potentially more dangerous than X-rays because gamma emitters can be taken inside the body.

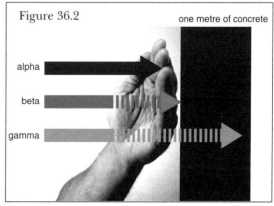

Figure 36.2

one metre of concrete

alpha

beta

gamma

Radiation risks

The risk from medical X-rays is extremely small. Modern radiography has reduced the exposure to very low levels. Doctors have replaced X-rays with safer imaging techniques like MRI scans, ultrasound scans and optical fibre scopes.

Radon is a particular danger

Radon gas is an alpha particle emitter. Long-term exposure to radon gas can cause lung cancer.

Radiation protection

1. Assume that there is no safe dose.
2. Keep all unavoidable doses as small as possible.
3. Any deliberate exposure – such as using radioisotopes to diagnose illness – should have some benefit that outweighs the danger.

SUMMARY

- Artificial radioactivity is radioactivity produced by bombarding non-radioactive isotopes with charged particles or neutrons.
- Radiation is used in medicine to treat cancers, diagnose diseases and produce images of the inside of the body.
- Radiation is used in industry in smoke detectors, as a power source, to detect leaks and check welds.
- Radiation is used in agriculture to preserve food, in agricultural research and pest control.
- Radiation is used in scientific research to date archaeological and geological materials and in radioactivation analysis.
- High levels of radiation kill cells.
- Long-term exposure to low-level radiation can lead to an increased incidence of cancer.

Chapter 37 – Nuclear Energy

Einstein showed that mass and energy are related by the equation: $E = mc^2$ where m is the mass of the body and c is the speed of light.

Conservation of Mass and Conservation of Energy taken separately do not work with nuclear reactions. Only Conservation of Mass-Energy combined works with nuclear reactions.

Mass-energy conservation was confirmed experimentally by Cockcroft and Walton:

$$^1_1H + ^7_3Li \Rightarrow ^4_2He + ^4_2He + Q$$

Cockcroft and Walton's experiment was the first direct confirmation of Einstein's prediction of the equivalence of mass and energy.

FISSION

Fission is the splitting of the nucleus of a heavy element into two or more smaller nuclei with the emission of neutrons and a large amount of energy.

Great amounts of energy are released in nuclear fission. Fission reactions can be caused by bombarding the nucleus with many different particles. Fission reactions caused by neutrons are the most important.

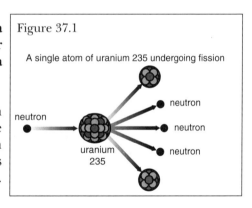

Figure 37.1

A single atom of uranium 235 undergoing fission

neutron

neutron

neutron

neutron

neutron

uranium 235

Why does fission happen with large atoms?

In large atoms the nucleons are relatively far apart from each other. The nuclear forces are not strong enough at these distances so that the repulsive forces between the protons tend to split the nucleus when a neutron hits it.

Uranium fission

U–238 undergoes radiative capture and very little fission.

Fission: $^{238}_{92}U + ^1_0n \Rightarrow$ 2 fragments + neutrons

Radiative capture: $^{238}_{92}U + ^1_0n \Rightarrow ^{238}_{92}U + ^1_0n +$ gamma

U–235 undergoes fission and little radiative capture.

Fission: $^{235}_{92}U + ^{1}_{0}n \Rightarrow 2$ fragments + neutrons

Radiative capture: $^{235}_{92}U + ^{1}_{0}n \Rightarrow ^{235}_{92}U + ^{1}_{0}n +$ gamma

Table 37.1

U–238	99·2%	mainly radiative capture	fission only with fast neutrons
U–235	0·7%	mainly fission	fission with fast and slow neutrons

For a **chain reaction** to take place each fission must produce at least one further fission.

A chain reaction is achieved by using uranium enriched with more U–235. Uncontrolled fission chain reactions use pure uranium 235 (U–235) or plutonium 239 (Pu–239).

NUCLEAR REACTORS

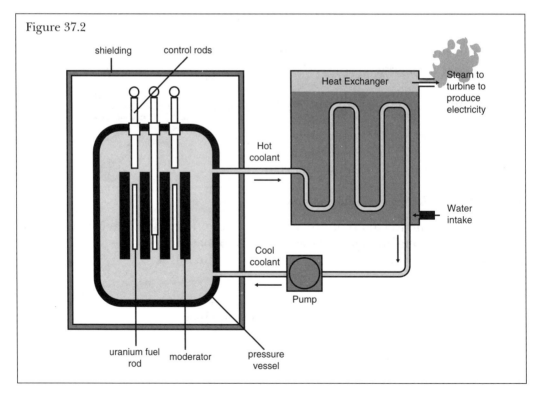

Figure 37.2

A nuclear reactor produces energy by fission in uranium fuel rods. The energy is used to boil water and drive a steam turbine generator set.

Fuel rods

The fuel rods are made from natural uranium, enriched in U–235.

Moderator

The moderator rapidly slows down neutrons to the energy that allows fission to happen. The moderator is a material like graphite or heavy water that slows down the neutrons without undergoing nuclear reactions.

Control rods

Control rods made from a neutron absorber like cadmium or boron steel. The rods are adjusted by raising or lowering them into the reactor core so that just one fission-producing neutron results from each fission. This controls the rate of fission.

Shielding

The reactor core is contained in a sealed vessel. Radiation does escape from the reactor core.

Heat exchanger

A nuclear reactor heats the boiler indirectly through a heat exchanger.

Problem

Calculate the energy released in the fission of 1 kg of uranium–235 when 200 MeV is emitted per fission event.

One mole of U–235 = 235 g

Number of moles in 1 kg = $\dfrac{1000}{235}$

Avogadro's number = $6\cdot023 \times 10^{23}$ per mole

Number of atoms in 1 kg of U–235 = $\left(\dfrac{1000}{235}\right) \times 6\cdot023 \times 10^{23}$

Total fission energy = $\left(\dfrac{1000}{235}\right) \times 6\cdot023 \times 10^{23} \times 200$ MeV
$= 51\cdot26 \times 10^{25}$ MeV

1 MeV = $1\cdot6 \times 10^{-19} \times 10^{6}$ J $= 1\cdot6 \times 10^{-13}$ J

$51\cdot26 \times 10^{25}$ MeV $= 8\cdot2 \times 10^{13}$ J

DANGERS OF FISSION REACTORS

1. Even though many reactors have a good safety record the potential for large-scale disaster is always present.

2. Disposal of nuclear waste including highly radioactive old nuclear reactors.
3. Reprocessing of used (spent) fuel rods from reactor cores.

FUSION

Fusion is the union of light nuclei to form a heavier nucleus with the emission of large amounts of energy.

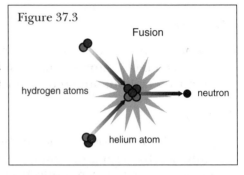

Figure 37.3

$$^2_1\text{H} + {}^2_1\text{H} \Rightarrow {}^3_2\text{He} + {}^1_0\text{n} + \text{energy}$$

Experimental fusion reactors

Experimental fusion reactors are attempting to produce sustained fusion of a plasma of hydrogen isotopes – a high-temperature mixture of deuterium and tritium. At temperatures of many hundred million degrees, all atoms are ionised and electrically charged. This plasma is kept in place in a doughnut-shaped tube called a tokamak with a powerful magnetic field.

Lithium metal is used as a heat exchanger because it is a good conductor of heat. Lithium also 'breeds' tritium when struck by neutrons. The tritium can later be extracted for use as fuel for further fusion.

Problem

Calculate the energy released when two protons, one neutron and two electrons combine to form a helium–3 atom of mass 3·01603 a.m.u.

neutron	1·008665 a.m.u.
proton	1·007825 a.m.u.
electron	0·0005486 a.m.u.

1 a.m.u. = $1·66 \times 10^{-27}$ kg

Mass 2p + 1n + 2e = 2(1·007825) + 1(1·008665) + 2(0·0005486)
= 3·0254122

Mass defect = 0·00938 a.m.u. = $0·01557 \times 10^{-27}$ kg

Energy = mc^2 = $(0·01557 \times 10^{-27})(3 \times 10^8)^2 = 1·4 \times 10^{-12}$ J

Controlled fusion is attractive as an energy source

1. Low fuel cost: 700 grams of deuterium could power a 200 MW station for 1 day.
2. Fuel is readily available from water. There is sufficient deuterium on earth to last for 2×10^4 million years at current energy consumption rates.

3. No radioactive wastes of long half-life to dispose of.
4. Fusion is not a chain reaction – it cannot get out of control.

SUMMARY

- Einstein's mass-energy equation ($E = mc^2$): When a small amount of matter seems to disappear, a large amount of energy is released in its place.
- Fission: the splitting of the nucleus of a heavy element into two or more fragments with the emission of neutrons and a large amount of energy.
- Slow or thermal neutrons are neutrons with energies of about 0·025 eV.
- Fast neutrons are neutrons with energies in excess of 1 keV.
- Chain reaction: a reaction where each fission event produces at least one further fission.
- Fusion: the union of light nuclei to form a heavier nucleus with the emission of large amounts of energy.

Chapter 38 – Inside the Atom (Option 1)

THE SEARCH FOR ORDER

Aristotle believed that all substances on earth were made from one or more of four basic substances – Earth, Air, Fire and Water.

Dalton's atomic theory stated that each atom has a characteristic mass and that atoms of elements are unchanged in chemical reactions. Dalton's atoms were solid and indivisible and all matter was made from them.

The discovery of the electron, proton and neutron and Rutherford's nuclear model of the atom changed this picture to an atom made up of a nucleus of protons and neutrons surrounded by orbiting electrons.

CONSERVATION OF MOMENTUM IN NUCLEAR REACTIONS

When a nucleus emits an α particle the nucleus recoils in the same way as a gun when a shot is fired.

Problem

Americium–241 emits an α particle with a velocity of 3×10^7 m s^{-1}. Calculate the recoil velocity of the resulting nucleus.

Nuclear equation: $^{241}_{95}\text{Am} \Rightarrow \, ^4_2\text{He} \, + \, ^{237}_{93}\text{Np}$

Momentum before emission = 0 (assume nucleus is at rest)
Momentum of α particle $m_1 v_1 = (4)(3 \times 10^7)$
Momentum of neptunium nucleus $m_2 v_2 = (237)(x)$
Conservation of momentum: momentum before = momentum after

$$0 = (4)(3 \times 10^7) + 237x$$

$$x = \frac{(4)(3 \times 10^7)}{(237)}$$

$$= 5 \cdot 06 \times 10^5 \text{ m s}^{-1}$$

THE NEUTRINO

When β particles are emitted by radioactive decay the process seemed to contradict Conservation of Energy and Conservation of Momentum. This led Pauli to suggest that another particle – a neutrino was emitted in the decay. When this is taken into account Energy and Momentum are conserved.

Neutrinos are also emitted in other nuclear reactions involving electrons. The neutrino ($^0_0\upsilon$) has zero charge and mass (like the photon) but has momentum and energy.

Problem

The following nuclear equation describes the emission of a beta particle from a nucleus. Use the values for the masses given to calculate the energy released in the reaction.

$$^1_0n \Rightarrow \, ^1_1p \, + \, ^0_{-1}e \, + \, ^0_0\upsilon$$

Mass of neutron = 1·008665 a.m.u.
Mass of proton = 1·007825 a.m.u.
Mass of electron = 0·0005486 a.m.u.
Mass of proton + Mass of electron = 1·0083736
Mass defect = Mass of neutron − (Mass of proton + Mass of electron)
= 1·008665 − 1·0083736 = 0·0002914

The mass defect produces an equivalent amount of energy about 271 keV. The emitted β particle has energy less than this. The rest is found in the energy of the neutrino.

Note: 1 a.m.u. is equivalent to an energy of 931 MeV

$$1 \text{ a.m.u.} = 1·660 \times 10^{-27} \text{ kg}$$

$$E = mc^2 = (1·66 \times 10^{-27})(3·0 \times 10^8)^2 \, \text{J}$$

$$= \frac{(1·660 \times 10^{-27})(3·0 \times 10^8)^2}{1·602 \times 10^{-19}} = 931 \text{ MeV}$$

CONSERVATION OF MASS–ENERGY

$E = mc^2$
where m is the mass of the body and c is the speed of light.

Problem

Calculate the energy released in the following nuclear reaction:

$$^2_1H + \, ^6_3Li \Rightarrow \, ^4_2He \, + \, ^4_2He + Q$$

Mass of deuteron = 2·014102 a.m.u.
Mass of lithium = 6·015125 a.m.u.
Sum of masses = 8·029227

$2 \times$ mass α particle = 8·005208 a.m.u.
Mass defect = 0·024019 a.m.u.
This is equivalent to 22·37 MeV

COCKCROFT AND WALTON SPLIT THE NUCLEUS

Mass-energy conservation was confirmed when a lithium target was bombarded by protons.

Cockcroft and Walton's experiment was the first direct confirmation of Einstein's prediction of the equivalence of mass and energy.

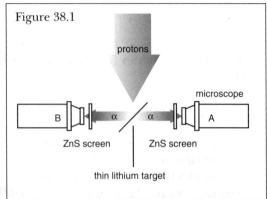

Figure 38.1

A MACHINE TO SMASH THE NUCLEUS

Linear accelerators

Cockcroft and Walton accelerated protons in a straight line – a linear accelerator.

Circular accelerators

A more compact way of accelerating particles was developed in 1930 by Lawrence. The cyclotron he invented was about the size of a dinner plate and had the following characteristics:

1. The particles are charged and can be accelerated by an electric field. A magnetic field at right angles to the direction of the particles forces them into a circular path.

2. Each time they come to the gap between the two semicircles the electric field accelerates them across the gap.

The frequency of the electric field ensures that this happens at the correct moment.

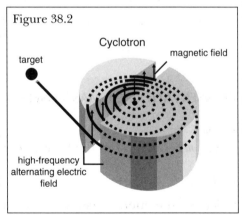

Figure 38.2

The **synchrocyclotron** adjusts the frequency to compensate for relativity effects and allow particles to accelerate to very high velocities.

The **synchrotron** adjusts the strength of the magnetic field to keep the particles moving in phase to adjust for relativity effects.

The 27 km circular accelerator in circumference built by CERN on the Swiss-French border near Geneva accelerates particles to energies of 500 GeV. CERN is the European Organisation for Nuclear Research (Conseil Européen pour la Recherche Nucléaire).

SUMMARY

- Nuclear reactions obey the law of conservation of momentum.
- The neutrino ($^0_0\upsilon$) has zero charge and mass but has momentum and energy.
- Conservation of mass-energy. $E = mc^2$.
- Cockcroft and Walton produced the first artificial splitting of a nucleus with an accelerated charged particle – a proton.
- Linear accelerators accelerated charged particles in a straight line.
- Circular Accelerators – cyclotrons, synchrocyclotrons and synchrotrons accelerate charged particles in circular paths.

Chapter 39 – Fundamental Particles (Option 1)

ANTIPARTICLES

The first antiparticle was discovered by Anderson in cosmic rays in 1932. He found a particle with the same mass as the electron but with a positive electric charge. This positive electron is the **positron**.

Converting energy into mass: pair production

Electron–positron pairs are produced when high-energy photons pass close to a nucleus – this is another example of mass–energy equivalence. The photon disappears and is replaced by two particles of equal mass and charge moving in opposite directions.

$$\gamma \Rightarrow e^- + e^+$$

This process is called pair production.

Problem

An electron and a positron are produced from a photon in the electric field of the nucleus. What is the minimum energy photon necessary for this?

$$\gamma \Rightarrow e^- + e^+$$

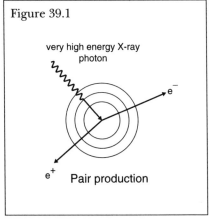

Figure 39.1

very high energy X-ray photon

e⁻

e⁺   Pair production

If we assume the two particles produced have zero kinetic energy:

mass of 2 electrons   = 2(0·0005486) a.m.u.

                   = 0·0010972 a.m.u.

Equivalent to energy   = 1·02 MeV

Annihilation

When an electron and a positron meet they annihilate each other and are replaced by two photons moving in opposite directions.

$$e^- + e^+ \Rightarrow \gamma + \gamma$$

We have already calculated the mass–energy of the electron-positron pair to be 1·02 MeV. As this produces 2 γ ray photons the energy of each photon must be 0·5 Mev.

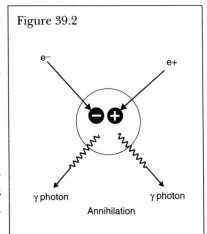

Figure 39.2

e⁻   e+

γ photon   γ photon
Annihilation

Antiprotons

It takes considerably more energy to produce a proton-antiproton pair because the mass of a proton is nearly 2,000 times that of an electron.

When a proton meets an antiproton they produce strange particles that in turn decay into other particles.

$$p^+ + p^- \Rightarrow \pi^+ + \pi^-$$

Table 39.1

Particle	Antiparticle
electron e^-	positron e^+
proton p^+	antiproton p^-
muon μ^-	antimuon μ^+

HIGH-ENERGY COLLISIONS

High-energy cosmic rays colliding with particles in the earth's atmosphere produce many strange particles such as the 'pion'.

Pions are formed when high-energy protons in the cosmic rays collide. The pion is a very short-lived particle and decays into another strange particle – a muon – and a neutrino in about 10^{-8} of a second.

Problem 1

A 1·8 GeV proton strikes a hydrogen nucleus (a proton) and produces a proton, a sigma hyperon and a K meson. Estimate the mass of the K meson if 1 GeV is accounted for in the other two particles.

$$p^+ + p^+ \Rightarrow p^+ + K^0 + \Sigma^+$$

$$0.8 \text{ GeV} = 0.8 \times 10^3 \text{ MeV}$$

This is equivalent to a mass of 0·85929 a.m.u.

Mass of p^+ = 1·007825 a.m.u.
Mass of Σ^+ = 1·277940 a.m.u.
Mass of 2 protons and mass equivalent of 0·8 GeV = 2·87494 a.m.u.
Mass of proton and sigma particle = 2·285765 a.m.u.
Mass of K meson = 0·589175 a.m.u.

Problem 2

A photon strikes a hydrogen nucleus (a proton) and produces a neutral lambda hyperon and a K meson. Calculate the minimum energy of the photon necessary for this reaction.

$\gamma + p^+ \Rightarrow K^+ + \Lambda$
Mass of $p^+ = 1 \cdot 007825$ a.m.u.
Mass of $K^+ = 0 \cdot 530344$ a.m.u.
Mass of $\Lambda^0 = 1 \cdot 198646$ a.m.u.
Mass of $K^+ + \Lambda^0 = 1 \cdot 72899$ a.m.u.
less mass of $p^+ = 1 \cdot 007825$ a.m.u.
Mass created = $0 \cdot 721165$ a.m.u.
$\Rightarrow$ Energy of photon must be at least 671 MeV

PROTON-PROTON COLLISIONS

Scientists produced strange particles with high-energy electron or proton collisions in accelerators. A large number of these particles have been produced. They are identical to the particles produced in cosmic rays.

Einstein's mass–energy equation works both ways – mass changes into energy but energy can also change into mass. When high-energy protons collide some of the enormous energy changes into mass.

Many other strange particles (with lifetimes of 10^{-6} to 10^{-20} seconds) are produced in high-energy proton collisions.
Examples:

Table 39.2

$p^+ + p^+ \Rightarrow p^+ + p^+ + (p^+ + p^-)$:	proton-antiproton pair produced
$p^+ + p^+ \Rightarrow p^+ + p^+ + \pi^0$:	neutral pion produced
$p^+ + p^+ \Rightarrow d^+ + \pi^+$:	deuteron (proton-neutron combination) and pion produced
$p^+ + p^+ \Rightarrow p^+ + \Sigma^+ + K^0$:	proton, sigma baryon and kaon (K meson) produced

FUNDAMENTAL FORCES OF NATURE

There are four fundamental forces in nature: the strong nuclear force, the weak nuclear force, the electromagnetic force and the gravitational force.

Electromagnetic and gravitational forces are easy to observe and have been known for a long time. They have an effect at a great distance and cause many of the forces we see in everyday life.

Strong and weak nuclear forces were not discovered until the twentieth century. These forces act on subatomic particles and only work at very short-range subatomic distances.

Table 39.3

Force	Relative Strength	Range	Purpose
Strong nuclear force	Very strong	Very short distances	Holds protons and neutrons together in nucleus
Weak nuclear force	Weaker than electromagnetic	Very short distances	Nuclear force involved in beta particle decay
Electromagnetic force	100 times weaker than strong nuclear force	Extends over great distances – obeys inverse square law	Holds atoms and molecules together
Gravitational force	Weakest of fundamental forces	Extends over enormous distances – obeys inverse square law	Holds universe together

THE ULTIMATE STRUCTURE OF MATTER?

Matter seems to be built from two groups of particles – **Hadrons** (nuclear particles) and **Leptons** (non-nuclear particles).

Hadrons are divided these into: **Baryons** ('heavy' particles) and **Mesons** (intermediate particles).

Baryons are a combination of three quarks.

Mesons are a combination of a quark and an antiquark.

Leptons are indivisible and are fundamental particles.

QUARKS

Murray Gell-Mann and George Zweig proposed a model that reduced all these heavy particles to combinations of three fundamental particles – Gell-Mann named the particles 'quarks'.

The three-quark model was soon found to be inadequate and was rapidly extended to six quarks (and six antiquarks). The quarks are named Up, Down, Strange, Charmed, Top and Bottom.

Quarks have a fractional electric charge – some have $\frac{1}{3}$ electron charge, others have $\frac{2}{3}$ electron charge.

Table 39.4

Quark	Charge	Antiquark	Charge
Up	$+\frac{2}{3}$	Up	$-\frac{2}{3}$
Down	$-\frac{1}{3}$	Down	$+\frac{1}{3}$
Strange	$-\frac{1}{3}$	Strange	$+\frac{1}{3}$
Charmed	$+\frac{2}{3}$	Charmed	$-\frac{2}{3}$
Top	$-\frac{1}{3}$	Top	$+\frac{1}{3}$
Bottom	$+\frac{2}{3}$	Bottom	$-\frac{2}{3}$

All heavy particles are combinations of quarks. Baryons are combinations of three quarks. Mesons are a quark-antiquark pair.

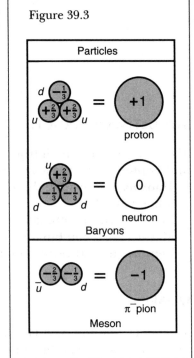

Figure 39.3

Baryons

Particle	Quarks	Charge
proton	uud	$\frac{2}{3} + \frac{2}{3} - \frac{1}{3} = +1$
neutron	udd	$\frac{2}{3} - \frac{1}{3} - \frac{1}{3} = 0$
Σ^+	uus	$\frac{2}{3} + \frac{2}{3} - \frac{1}{3} = +1$
Σ^-	dds	$-\frac{1}{3} - \frac{1}{3} - \frac{1}{3} = -1$

Mesons

Particle	Quark-antiquark	Charge
π^+	$u\bar{d}$	$\frac{2}{3} + \frac{1}{3} = +1$
π^-	$\bar{u}d$	$-\frac{2}{3} - \frac{1}{3} = -1$
K^+	$u\bar{s}$	$\frac{2}{3} + \frac{1}{3} = +1$
K^-	$\bar{u}s$	$-\frac{2}{3} - \frac{1}{3} = -1$

Matter is now seen as made up of leptons and baryons. Leptons are fundamental particles and are not subject to the strong nuclear force. Baryons are all composed of quarks. The fundamental particles are six quarks and also six leptons.

Table 39.5

Six quarks	Six leptons	Six antiquarks	Six antileptons
Up	Electron	Up	Positron
Down	Electron neutrino	Down	Electron antineutrino
Strange	Negative muon	Strange	Positive muon
Charmed	Muon neutrino	Charmed	Muon antineutrino
Top	Negative tau	Top	Positive tau
Bottom	Tau neutrino	Bottom	Tau antineutrino

SUMMARY

- Cosmic radiation is radiation coming from outside the earth.
- Electron-positron pairs are produced when high-energy photons pass close to a nucleus.
- An electron and a positron annihilate each other and are replaced by two photons moving in opposite directions.

- The greater the energy of a beam of protons the greater the masses of the particles produced.
- A particle of energy E in a collision can, in theory, produce a particle of mass $\frac{E}{c^2}$.
- There are four fundamental forces in nature: the strong nuclear force, the weak nuclear force, the electromagnetic force and the gravitational force.
- Baryons are all large mass particles, are influenced by the strong nuclear force and are a combination of three quarks.
- Mesons are particles with masses between the electron and the proton, are influenced by the strong nuclear force and are a combination of a quark and an antiquark.
- Leptons are fundamental particles that are not influenced by the strong nuclear force.
- Quarks have a fractional electric charge of $\frac{1}{3}$ or $\frac{2}{3}$ electron charge.

- The fundamental particles are six quarks and also six leptons.

AN ROINN OIDEACHAIS AGUS EOLAÍOCHTA

LEAVING CERTIFICATE EXAMINATION, SAMPLE PAPER

MAY 2001

PHYSICS — HIGHER LEVEL

3 HOURS DURATION

Answer **three** questions from section A and **five** questions from section B.

Data

Gravitational constant = 6.7×10^{-11} N m^2 kg^{-2}

Radius of the earth = 6.4×10^6 m

Mass of the earth = 6.0×10^{24} kg

Speed of light in a vacuum = 3.0×10^8 m s^{-1}

Speed of sound in air = 340 m s^{-1}

SECTION A (120 marks)

Answer **three** questions from this section.
Each question carries 40 marks.

1. In investigating simple harmonic motion, a simple pendulum was set up so that it could swing freely about a fixed point. The length of the pendulum was measured. The pendulum was allowed to swing through a small angle and the time for 25 oscillations, t, was found. This procedure was repeated for a series of values of the length l. the data obtained are shown in the table.

l/cm	40·0	50·0	60·0	70·0	80·0	90·0	100·0
t/s	31·1	34·5	38·8	42·5	44·4	47·8	49·6

Is the period of the pendulum proportional to its length? Justify your answer. (7)
Draw a suitable graph on graph paper to illustrate the relationship between the period and the length. Hence determine a value for the acceleration due to gravity, g. (21)
How is the pendulum set up so that it swings freely? (6)
Explain why the pendulum is allowed to swing through only a small angle. (6)

2. The following is part of a report given by a student of an experiment to measure the wavelength of monochromatic light. 'The apparatus was arranged so that a number of bright images could be observed. The angular position θ for each of

163

these images was determined. The data obtained are shown in the table. The diffraction grating had 600 lines per mm.'

n	2	1	0	1	2
$\theta/°$	45.0	20.4	0.0	20.7	45.2

Describe, with the aid of a diagram, how the student might have obtained the data. (12)

Use the data to calculate a value for the wavelength of the light. (12)

Explain why it is not possible to get more than five bright images with this diffraction grating. (10)

Name two factors that would affect the accuracy of the experiment. (6)

3. A student investigated the variation of the fundamental frequency f of a stretched string with its length l and the following data was obtained.

$l/$m	0.2	0.3	0.4	0.5	0.6	0.7	0.8
$f/$Hz	675	455	335	273	230	193	173

Describe, with the aid of a diagram, how the student might have obtained the data. (12)

How would the student have known that the string was vibrating at its fundamental frequency? (6)

Explain why the tension in the string should be kept constant during the investigation. (3)

Draw a suitable graph to illustrate the relationship between the fundamental frequency and the length of the stretched string. (13)

From your graph, estimate the length of the string when its fundamental frequency is 256 Hz. (6)

4. The current I through a component was measured for a range of different values of potential difference V applied across it. The recorded data are shown in the table.

$V/$N	0.0	1.0	2.0	3.0	4.0	5.0	6.0
$I/$A	0.0	0.20	0.28	0.35	0.38	0.39	0.40

Draw a suitable circuit diagram to obtain the data. (9)

Describe how the data could be obtained from your circuit. (6)

Plot a graph of the current against the potential difference for this component. (12)

Referring to your graph, discuss how the current varies with the potential difference. Your answer should make reference to Ohm's law and the resistance of the component. (13)

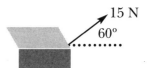

SECTION B (280 marks)

Answer **five** questions from this section.
Each question carries 56 marks.

5. Answer all of the following parts.
   (i)   A force of 15 N acts on a box as shown.
         What is the horizontal component of the force?   (6)
   (ii) State Hooke's law.   (6)
   (iii) 100 litres of carbon dioxide gas at an atmospheric pressure of 1×10^5 Pa
         was pumped into a gas cylinder of volume 0·5 litres. What is the pressure in
         the gas cylinder?   (6)
   (iv) What is meant by the U-value of a structure?   (6)
   (v)   What is the shortest wavelength of sound that can be heard in air by a
         person given that the frequency response of the ear ranges from 20 Hz to
         20 kHz?   6)
   (vi) A tin whistle has a fundamental frequency of 256 Hz. What is the frequency
         of the third harmonic?   (6)
   (vii) A capacitor is marked 100 μF. What is the energy stored in the capacitor
         when it is connected to a 6 V supply?   (6)
   (viii) If the peak voltage of an a.c. source is 15 V, calculate its rms value.   (7)
   (ix) Distinguish between leptons and baryons.   (7)
         OR
   (ix) What is the physical principle on which a loudspeaker is based.   (7)

6. Isaac Newton developed the theory of gravitation at the end of the seventeenth
   century. According to this theory, what is gravity? State Newton's law of universal
   gravitation.   (12)
   What is meant by centripetal force? Describe how you would demonstrate the
   effect of centripetal force.   (12)
   A satellite of mass m orbits the earth in a circular orbit at a constant height h
   above the earth's surface. Show that the period T of the satellite is given by

   $$T^2 = \frac{4\pi^2 \, (R + h)^3}{GM}$$

   where R is the radius of the earth, G is the gravitational constant and M is the
   mass of the earth.   (15)
   A communications satellite is usually in an orbit such that it appears stationary
   above a point on the earth's equator. What is the period of such a satellite? (6)
   Calculate the height of such a communications satellite above the surface of the
   earth.   (11)

7. Explain what is meant by the term *power.*   (6)
   Microwave ovens are common in many kitchens. In such an oven microwave
   energy is absorbed by the water present in food and is converted to heat.
   An electrician tested the efficiency of a microwave oven, which had a power
   rating of 650 W, as follows.

A plastic jug, of negligible heat capacity, containing 500 cm³ of water at 20°C was placed in the microwave oven. The oven was switched on at full power. After two minutes the temperature of the water had risen to 54°C. Calculate the energy absorbed by the water. Hence determine the efficiency of the microwave oven.

(24)

Microwaves are continuously reflected off the walls of the oven. Interference occurs where they meet.
What effect might this have on the cooking of food placed in the oven?
Explain how this effect is lessened by using a turntable.   (12)

The microwaves produced in the oven have a frequency of 2·45 GHz. Calculate their wavelength.   (9)

Give another use for microwave radiation.   (5)

8. (a)   Draw a ray diagram to show the formation of a virtual image in a concave mirror.   (6)
   A dentist holds a concave mirror of focal length 25 mm at a distance of 20 mm from a cavity in a tooth. Where is the image of the cavity and what is its magnification?   (12)
   Explain why a concave mirror should not be used as a rear-view mirror in a car.   (6)
  (b) The focal length, hence the power, of a diverging lens can be determined by placing it in contact with a converging lens such that the two lenses together act as a converging lens.

   In an experiment to measure the focal length of a diverging lens, a converging lens of power 0·05 m⁻¹ is placed in contact with it. The combination has a power of + 0·02m⁻¹.
      Describe how the focal length of the combination could have been determined experimentally. What is the focal length of the diverging lens?

(21)

   Use a ray diagram to show how short sight can be corrected using a diverging lens.   (11)

9. Describe, with the aid of a circuit diagram, how a potential divider can provide a variable voltage from a fixed voltage supply.   (9)
   Derive an equation for the effective resistance of two resistors joined in series.

(12)

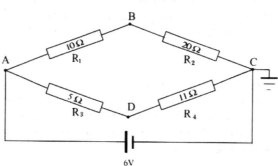

The diagram shows a Wheatstone bridge circuit that is almost balanced, with the point C earthed.
Calculate the current flowing through the resistor R_1 and hence calculate the potential at the point B. (12)
What is the potential at the point D? (6)
If a galvanometer is connected between the points B and D, what is the direction of the current flowing through it? (6)
What value of the resistance of R_4 would make the galvanometer read zero? (5)
Give two practical uses for a Wheatstone bridge. (6)

10. Outline the contribution of Michael Faraday to the development of the understanding of electricity in the nineteenth century. (12)
State the laws of electromagnetic induction. Describe an experiment to demonstrate one of these laws. (21)
The vertical component of the magnetic flux density of the earth's magnetic field is $7 \cdot 9 \times 10^{-6}$ T. A train is travelling at 100 km h^{-1} along two continuous horizontal metal tracks, which are 2 m apart. What would be the reading on a voltmeter connected across the tracks? (17)
Why would the voltmeter read zero if it were attached across two ends of one of the train's axles? (6)

11. Give the composition of the proton and the neutron in terms of quarks. (6)
A quark and an antiquark combine to form a meson. The π-meson family is made up of u and d quarks only. A π-meson can be positively charged, negatively charged or neutral.
Give the quark composition of each of the three types of π-meson. (12)

A beam of charged π-mesons is travelling with a speed $v = 0 \cdot 3c$ (where c is the speed of light in a vacuum). What is the mean distance travelled before decay? The mean life of a π-meson is $2 \cdot 6 \times 10^{-8}$ s. (6)

List three of the fundamental forces of nature and give one property of each. (18)
Describe how particle accelerators have increased our knowledge of particle physics. (14)

OR

11. How would you demonstrate that a current-carrying conductor experiences a force when placed in a magnetic field? (9)

A moving-coil galvanometer has a resistance of 100 Ω and it gives a full-scale deflection when a current of 1 mA flows through it. It is converted to a voltmeter with a full-scale deflection of 1 V by placing a resistor in series with it. Calculate the resistance of the resistor. (12)

Draw a labelled diagram of a simple d.c. motor and explain how it works. (18)

Transformers have many applications in the home. Give two examples. (6)

List two factors that affect the efficiency of a transformer. (6)

A transformer is used to give an output voltage of 2·2 kV when connected to the mains (230 V).

Calculate the turns-ratio of the coils in the transformer. (5)

12. *Irish Times: 19 February 2000*

Pupils from 13 schools at risk from radon

An Irish secondary school has radon gas more than thirteen times the safety level set by the Radiological Protection Institute of Ireland (RPII). It is among 13 schools whose radon levels are so high that immediate remedial action needs to be taken.

The safety limit for radon gas, which can cause lung cancer, is 200 becquerels per cubic metre.

The school's levels were measured at 2,688 becquerels in a survey carried out by the RPII last year.

Radon is a naturally occurring radioactive gas, which is formed by the radioactive decay of uranium, which is present in all rocks and soils. If the gas enters an enclosed space it can rise to unacceptably high levels.

(i) Name the physical quantity that is measured in becquerels and give the definition of this unit. (12)

(ii) Explain the term *radioactive decay*. (9)

(iii) Outline how the level of radon gas could have been measured. (9)

(iv) According to the above article, radon gas can cause lung cancer. How can radon gas cause lung cancer? (12)

(v) Suggest what remedial action could be taken to reduce the level of radon gas in the school. (9)

(vi) Name another source of natural radiation. (5)

AN ROINN OIDEACHAIS AGUS EOLAÍOCHTA

LEAVING CERTIFICATE EXAMINATION, SAMPLE PAPER

MAY 2001

PHYSICS — ORDINARY LEVEL

3 HOURS DURATION

Answer **three** questions from section A and **five** questions from section B.

SECTION A (120 marks)

Answer **three** questions from this section.
Each question carries 40 marks.

1. You have carried out an experiment to verify the principle of conservation of momentum.
   Draw a labelled diagram of the apparatus you used. (12)
   Describe how you measured the velocity. (9)
   As well as measuring velocity, what other measurement is required? (6)
   How would you know that the principle of conservation of momentum was verified? (9)
   Give one precaution you took to make the experiment accurate. (4)

2. You are asked to measure the refractive index of a substance using Snell's law.
   List the apparatus that you need for this experiment. (6)
   Draw a diagram to show how the apparatus is arranged. (6)
   Describe how the angle of incidence and the angle of refraction are measured. (12)

   The following table gives the data a student recorded in this experiment.
   Why was there a need for more than one set of readings? (3)
   Use the data to find the refractive index of the substance. (13)

Angle of incidence/°	20	40	60
Angle of refraction/°	13	25	35

3. A student measured the variation of the resistance R of a coil of wire with temperature θ and the following data was produced.

$\theta/°C$	10	20	30	40	50	60	70	80
R/Ω	3·8	4·1	4·4	4·8	5·0	5·3	5·7	6·0

List the apparatus used.   (9)
Draw a labelled diagram to show how the apparatus was arranged.   (6)
How was the temperature changed?   (6)
Draw a graph of resistance against temperature. Put temperature on the
horizontal axis.   (12)

The coil was left in a warm room and its resistance was found to be 4·2 Ω. From
your graph, estimate the temperature of the room.   (7)

4. The diagram shows the circuit used by a student to investigate the variation of
    current with potential difference for a metallic conductor.

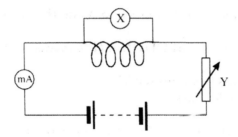

Name the apparatus X. What does it measure?   (6)
Name the apparatus Y. What does it do?   (6)

The following table shows the values obtained for the current *I* and the potential
difference *V* during the experiment.

I/mA	100	200	300	400	500	600	700	800
V/V	0·6	1·1	1·9	2·4	3·0	3·4	4·0	4·9

Draw a graph of current against potential difference. Put current on the
horizontal axis.   (12)
Explain how your graph verifies that the conductor obeys Ohm's law.   (7)
From your graph, calculate the resistance of the conductor.   (9)

SECTION B (280 marks)

Answer **five** questions from this section.
Each question carries 56 marks.

5. Answer *all* of the following parts.
    (i)   A car slows down when the driver applies the brakes. Rewrite the sentence
          below choosing words from the following list:

          potential   friction   gravity   heat   newtons   speed

'The brakes used the force of _____ to change the kinetic energy of the car to _____.'   (6)

(ii) Explain why it is more likely to be frosty on a clear night than on a cloudy night.   (6)

(iii) Convert 27°C to Kelvin.   (6)

(iv) Which two of the following devices make use of total internal reflection?

floodlights   car rear-view mirrors   prisms in binoculars   endoscopes (6)

(v) The diagram shows a spectrometer. Name two of the parts labelled A, B, C and D.   (6)

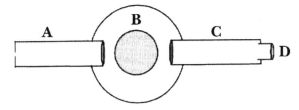

(vi) A teenager tuned a radio to 2FM. Which of the following devices was adjusted?

resistor   capacitor   diode   loudspeaker   (6)

(vii) What is a semiconductor?   (6)

(viii) What happens to a beam of electrons when it enters a magnetic field at right angles?   (7)

(ix) Give two properties of X-rays.   (7)

6. State Newton's first law of motion.   (9)

A car of mass 1,200 kg is travelling at a constant speed along a level road. Draw a diagram showing the forces acting on the car.   (9)

The car hits a wall at a speed of 20 m s^{-1} and is stopped in 0·2 s.
Calculate (i) the acceleration of the car during the collision,
              (ii) the force acting on the car during the collision.   (15)

The driver was not wearing a seatbelt and so hit the steering wheel when the car was suddenly brought to a stop. Using Newton's laws of motion, explain how wearing a seatbelt could have prevented this from happening.   (15)

Calculate the energy of the car as it hit the wall. What happens to this energy after the car hits the wall?   (8)

$(v = u + at;\ F = ma;\ E_k = {}^1\!/_2 mv^2)$

7. What is meant by *temperature?*   (6)
Describe an experiment to compare the rates of conduction of heat through a
number of different solids.   (15)
Name two other ways in which heat can be transferred.   (6)

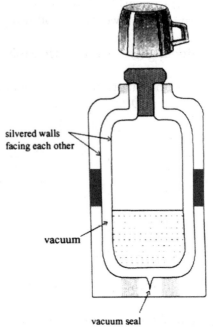

The spongy material in a wetsuit keeps
the layer of water near the swimmer's skin
from moving. Explain how a wetsuit can
keep a swimmer warm.   (12)

A vacuum flask (thermos flask) is
designed to keep a liquid in it at a fixed
temperature.
By referring to the diagram, explain how   silvered walls
the flask can keep the liquid at a fixed   facing each other
temperature.   (17)

8. Describe how you would demonstrate the
formation of a real image by a converging
lens.   (8)

vacuum

Explain, with the aid of diagrams, how the
human eye can form a sharp image of (i)
a near object, (ii) a distant object.   (12)

vacuum seal

The distance between the centre of the eye-lens system and the retina is 2 cm.
What is the focal length of the eye-lens system when viewing an object that is
50 cm away?   (12)
Calculate the power of the eye-lens system when viewing this object.   (9)

Name a common defect of vision in the human eye. Explain how wearing
spectacles can correct this defect.   (15)
$$\left(\frac{1}{f}=\frac{1}{u}+\frac{1}{v}; \quad P=\frac{1}{f}\right)$$

9. Describe an experiment to demonstrate the heating effect of an electric current.
                              (12)
The diagram shows part of the lighting circuit in a room.

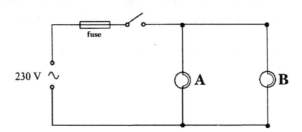

fuse

230 V

A   B

A is a 75 W lamp. The switch is closed. Calculate the current flowing through lamp A.   (12)
The current flowing through the fuse is 0·76 A. What is the current flowing through lamp B?   (6)
Calculate the resistance of lamp B.   (9)
Explain how the fuse acts as a safety device in this circuit.   (6)

An electric kettle is rated 3 kW. On average, the kettle is on for 30 minutes each day. How many units of electricity does the kettle use each day? How much does it cost to use the kettle each day, when one unit of electricity costs 8·36p? (11) ($P = VI$; $V = RI$)

10. What is the difference between a permanent magnet and an electromagnet? (6)
Magnets have many uses in the home. Give an application in the home of (i) a permanent magnet, (ii) an electromagnet.   (6)

The needle of a magnet compass is a permanent magnet.
Explain why one end of the compass needle turns toward a piece of iron placed nearby.   (6)
Explain why a nearby electric current disturbs a compass needle.   (6)

A solenoid is connected to a cell as shown. Copy this diagram into your answer-book and sketch its magnetic field.   (9)

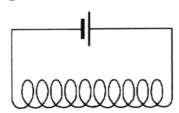

Explain the term *electromagnetic induction.*   (9)
A magnetic field and a coil of wire can be used to generate electricity. Describe, with the aid of a diagram, how you could demonstrate this.   (14)

11. Three types of radiation are α, β, γ.
Match each of the following descriptions with the correct type of radiation.
  (i) short wavelength electromagnetic radiation
  (ii) a particle consisting of two protons and two neutrons
(iii) a fast-moving electron.   (9)

Radon-222 is a radioactive gas that can seep into buildings from underground rocks. It undergoes the following nuclear reaction.

$$^{222}_{86}\text{Rn} \rightarrow {}^{218}_{84}\text{Po} + {}^{4}_{2}\text{He}$$

What type of radiation is emitted by radon-222?   (6)

Explain what is meant by the *half-life* of a radioactive material. (6)
The half-life of radon-222 is 4 days. The activity of a sample of radon-222 is measured as 520 Bq. Estimate the activity of the radon-222 sample after 12 days. (9)

Outline the principle of operation of a detector of ionising radiation. (9)
Describe how you would measure the activity of a sample of radon-222. (9)
Why is it important to control the level of radon gas in a building? (9)

12. The following is an extract from a Health and Safety Authority leaflet on Noise Exposure.

IS YOUR WORK MAKING YOU DEAF?
Forty of every hundred workers who have worked all their lives at high noise levels (90 dB(A) decibels) will, at the age of 65 years, find it difficult to hear other people talking. Some of these workers will even be deaf.
This deafness means that you can hear sounds but they are totally distorted or 'muffled'.

This type of deafness is incurable.
This type of deafness can be prevented.

How can I be protected?
If you are exposed to continuous loud noise at work the 'European Communities (Protection of Workers) (Exposure to Noise) Regulations 1990' set out what your employers must do to protect you from noise exposure. They must assess, measure and control noise and supply hearing protection as appropriate.

Assessing Noise
The level of noise to note is 85 dB(A).
If it is necessary to communicate by shouting at a distance of 2 m, the noise level may well be 85 dB(A). A specially trained person should, therefore, measure the noise level.

(i) What is noise? (6)
(ii) How might a person's hearing be affected by exposure to high noise levels? (6)
(iii) Name a source of high noise level that might be found in the workplace. (6)
(iv) What physical quantity is measured in decibels? (6)
(v) What is the dB(A)? (6)
(vi) How are noise levels measured? (6)
(vii) What must employers do if their workers are exposed to high noise levels? (6)
(viii) Where else, other than at work, might you be exposed to high noise levels? (6)
(ix) Explain the term *frequency response of the ear.* (8)